KV-042-848

Contents

Acknowledgments

We are most grateful to the Joseph Rowntree Foundation for asking us to carry out the work which we report in the following pages. We would like to thank, especially, the experts who provided national overviews, read the work in draft and answered our many queries: Claire Leconte and Paul and Sophie Craddock in France, Lisbeth Flising in Sweden and Michelle Seligson in the USA.

Peter Moss, Pat Petrie, Gill Poland

UNIVERSITY OF PLYMOUTH
LIBRARY SERVICES

Item No.	413390 2
Class No.	370.91 MOS
Contl No.	0 86155 2121

WITHDRAWN
FROM
UNIVERSITY OF PLYMOUTH

90 0413390 2

Rethinking school:
ternational perspectives

sc

Pat Petrie and Gill Poland

YOUTH • WORK • PRESS

JR
JOSEPH
ROWNTREE
FOUNDATION

First published in Great Britain in 1999 by Youth Work Press, the publishing imprint of the National Youth Agency.

17–23 Albion Street, Leicester LE1 6GD.

Tel: 0116.285.3700. Fax: 0116.285.3777.

E-mail: nya@nya.org.uk Website: http://www.nya.org.uk

Published for the Joseph Rowntree Foundation by Youth Work Press

© Youth Work Press and Joseph Rowntree Foundation 1999

ISBN 0 86155 212 1

Price: £12.95

The Joseph Rowntree Foundation has supported this project as part of its programme of research and innovative development projects, which it hopes will be of value to policy-makers, practitioners and service users. The facts presented and views expressed in this report, however, are those of the authors and not necessarily those of the Foundation.

Any views expressed in this report are solely those of the authors and contributors and not necessarily of Youth Work Press or the National Youth Agency.

Cover design: Sanjay Kukadia. Photos courtesy Marrissa Khan, Sebastian Buccheri and Jim Preston.

Printed by Joseph Ball, Leicester

1 Introduction

France, Sweden and the United States: similarities and differences

This report responds to a brief from the Joseph Rowntree Foundation

> 'to draw together and assess evidence from outside the UK of ways in which, and in what circumstances, the involvement of school beyond the conventional boundaries of formal education (as understood in the UK) can generate benefits (however defined) for children/young people, their families and local communities.'

The background to this brief includes a report for the Joseph Rowntree Foundation, *School Inclusion* (Ball, 1998), mapping the range of activities which can link school, family and community in the UK; and work being undertaken by the government's Social Exclusion Unit, Schools Plus, considering school-based activities, outside school hours, as a means of alleviating educational under-achievement.

We agreed to focus on three countries: France, Sweden and the United States (US). These national case studies of relations and collaborations between school, family and community are set in the wider context of approaches to children's services; social and economic conditions; and paradigms of childhood – the understandings of childhood within each country.

In some important ways the three countries have much in common, with each other and with the UK. They are all wealthy. Employment among women is high and has been growing. The proportion of children in the population is

declining, and fertility rates are at, or below, replacement level (Table 1). They are all, in diverse ways, multi-ethnic societies. All experience increasing diversity in family life – decreasing numbers of married parents and increasing lone, cohabiting and repartnered parents.

But on certain key parameters, to which we now turn, the three countries differ markedly. It is because they contrast strongly that we have chosen them.

Population

The three countries have very different sized populations. The US has a larger child population, proportionately, and a substantially higher fertility rate than France or Sweden (Table 1). It has a larger and more diverse minority ethnic population, and the highest level of lone parent families (29 per cent in 1991, compared with 21 per cent for the UK, 18 per cent for Sweden and 13 per cent for France (both 1990) (Bradshaw et al, 1996: Table 2.1.)).

Government

The US has a federal constitution. States exercise extensive legislative and executive power and responsibility, especially in education and human services. By contrast, Sweden and France have been centralised nation states. But Sweden, like other Scandinavian countries, has entered a period of decentralisation from national to local government. France has also been engaged in decentralisation, although to a lesser extent than Sweden.

The Welfare State

The three countries present three different types of welfare states (Esping-Andersen, 1990), in terms of tradition, values, purpose, extent, structure and

Table 1 – some key demographic and economic indices for France, Sweden, the UK and the US

	France	Sweden	UK	US
Population ('000s)(1996)	58,380	8,901	58,782	265,557
% of population under 15	19.3	18.8	19.3	21.7
Total fertility rate (1996)	1.72	1.61	1.7	2.06
Infant mortality as % of live births (1996)	0.49	0.4	0.62 (1995)	0.8 (1995)
Health expenditure as % of GDP (1996)	9.7	7.3	6.9	14.0
% of 17 to 34-year-olds in tertiary education (1995)	13.6	9.2	9.3	16.0
Expenditure per student (US dollars converted using PPPs[1]) (1994)	4,700	5,680	4,340 (state funded schools only)	7,790
Educational expenditure } Public as % of GDP (1994) } Total	5.6 / 6.2	6.6 / 6.7	4.6 / No information	4.9 / 6.6
Female labour force participation (1996)	59.9	73.7	66.4	71.0
Part-time employment as % of total – women (1996)	29.5	39.0	44.8	26.9
Women's expected years in employment, 25–64	23.1	32.5	26.2	26.4
Unemployment rate (1996)	12.3	8.1	8.2	5.3
Government expenditure as % of GDP	51.6 (1996)	63.8 (1995)	42.3 (1994)	34.3 (1995)
Total tax receipts as % of GDP (1995)	44.5	49.7	35.3	27.9
Disposable income of average production worker, married with two children, as % of gross pay (1995)	72.6	67.4	73.3	74.2
Per capita GDP in $ using PPPs (1996)	20,533	19,258	18,636	27,821

Sources: OECD, 1997a, 1998

1 PPPs stand for Purchasing Power Parities. These are the rate of currency conversion which eliminates the difference in price levels between countries. These provide the best comparison of actual living standards between countries.

content. Sweden presents the Nordic model committed to redistribution, universality and high levels of benefits and services; France the conservative corporatist model, depending heavily on insurance arrangements related to labour market status; and the US the liberal regime, in which the welfare state has a limited and residual public responsibility. These differences are reflected in tax levels and government expenditure, which are much higher in Sweden and France than in the US (Table 1).

The differences in both government and welfare state produce more uniform national systems of services for children in France and Sweden (even with increasing decentralisation), compared with the diversity at state and local levels in the US.

Education

There are several significant variations between the education systems of the three countries. Here we will mention three.

First, **the age at which children enter the education system**. In Sweden, all early childhood services come within the education system and children have a legal entitlement to a publicly-funded service from the age of 12 months (before which time parents are assumed to be taking paid parental leave). However, early participation in the education system is not synonymous with schooling; children attend either nurseries or family day care until they are between 6 and 7 years of age. Schooling is available for all 6-year-olds and obligatory at age 7. In France, the youngest children go to services such as nurseries and family day care that are part of the welfare system. From around two and a half years, they are admitted to nursery schools within the education system with many 2-year-olds and nearly all 3 to 6-year-olds attending,

mostly full-time. Finally, in the US, children mainly do not enter the education system until kindergarten, often part time, at age 4 or 5 years. Nationally, the Department of Health has the biggest interest in early childhood services, including Head Start, child care, child welfare, health and mental health services, although at state level education departments may be more involved.

Second, the US has a higher **proportion of its population in tertiary education** than either France or Sweden (Table 1). In 1995, young people aged 17 could expect to spend on average 3.3 years in tertiary education in the US, 2.5 years in France and 1.8 years in Sweden (OECD, 1997a). Educational expenditure, as a proportion of GDP, is similar for all three countries (Table 1), but France and Sweden spend more proportionately on primary and secondary education (4.3 per cent and 4.5 per cent of GDP) than the US (3.9 per cent) and less on tertiary education (1.6 per cent and 1.1 per cent, compared with 2.4 per cent).

Finally, **expenditure per student** is higher in the US than in either France or Sweden across all levels of education (Table 1).

The United Nations Convention on the Rights of the Child

As will become apparent, these three countries have different understandings of the child and childhood. This variation is also reflected in their differing positions regarding the UN Convention on the Rights of the Child. France generally adopts an intermediate position, between Sweden and other Nordic countries which adhere closely to the resolutions of the Convention, and countries like the UK and Germany which more often disregard them (Bartley, 1998). Worldwide, only two countries have not signed the Convention – the US and Somalia.

Labour markets and employment

All three countries have high and growing levels of female, and maternal, employment. However, the female labour force participation rate is substantially higher in Sweden and the US than in France (Table 1). In 1995, 63 per cent of women in France with a child under 17 were employed, compared with 69 per cent in the US, and 75 per cent of Swedish women with a child under 7. Swedish women are more likely to work part time.

Taking account of working hours and holidays, American workers spend substantially longer at work than their French or Swedish counterparts. For example, in the early 1990s American workers averaged 12 days holiday a year compared with 27 days in Sweden (quoted in Hochschild, 1997). French and Swedish workers, on the other hand, suffer higher rates of unemployment than do Americans (Table 1).

Legal entitlements for working parents are more extensive in Sweden than in France or the US, and include paid parental leave and leave to care for sick children, the right to work reduced hours and publicly-funded child care for children from 1 to 12 years of age. French parents' rights are less extensive, but exceed those available to American parents.

Economies

On the basis of per capita GDP, the US is by far the wealthiest of the three countries (Table 1). Its economy is driven by a form of capitalism, sometimes referred to as Anglo-Saxon,

> commonly regarded as the most individualistic and libertarian of all. Its financial system is highly market based; the returns it requires are very high ... Unions are weak, employment regulation minimal and the turnover of workers is high as companies trim their staff to market demands ... [T]here is little spending on social welfare and levels of corporate and personal taxation are low ... However the US has proved an effective generator of jobs – although by European standards they are astonishingly poorly paid (Hutton, 1995: 258–9).

Globally, such neo-liberal capitalism, which values competitiveness and flexibility, has exerted increasing influence, and France and Sweden have both come under pressure to adapt to it. However, there has been resistance in both countries to calls for greater labour market 'flexibility' and wholesale welfare reform. Compared with the US, trade unions remain stronger (especially in Sweden) with collective bargaining an important feature of industrial relations, the welfare state retains a universal orientation, and the role of the market, especially in the social field, remains a contested issue. Jobs have, however, proven harder to generate, in part, it is argued, because the workforce is relatively 'inflexible' by American standards.

Inequality

Many indicators in Table 1 might lead the reader to assume that the US enjoys the best social conditions and has least cause for social concern. GDP and expenditure on health and education are all high. Yet it figures poorly on many socio-economic indicators, epitomised by its relatively high infant mortality rate compared with Sweden (Table 1). A pervading theme of the US case study is a deep unease about the state of the nation, and especially its children and young people.

What accounts for this apparent discrepancy? American capitalism generates enormous economic outputs and has placed the US at the cutting edge of technological developments, but it also seems to generate enormous economic inequalities. Huge expenditure on health (Table 1) is due in part to the major role of private health care. A quarter of educational expenditure is private (mostly in the tertiary sector (OECD, 1997a, Table B1.1c)), compared with 9 per cent in France and 2 per cent in Sweden (ibid., Table B1.1a). The tax take in the US may be low compared with France and Sweden, but there is little difference in the disposable incomes of blue-collar workers with children, in part because of redistributive social policies in France and Sweden (Table 1).

A recent analysis of low wages and poverty in Europe and North America (Marx, 1999) shows that the US has both the highest poverty rate among the population of working age, and the highest proportion of low paid workers (Figure 1). Sweden is among the three countries with the lowest poverty rate, taking account of both indices, with France in the middle while the UK approaches the levels of the US[2]. The US appears to face a double problem: low pay for those in work (where it affects one in four workers), and low income for those not in work:

> One finds a poverty rate of 40 per cent for non-employed Americans, which is about twice as high as for any of the European countries, except the UK, and about four times as high as for countries like Belgium,

Figure 1: Source Marx 1999

Denmark, Finland and Norway (Marx, 1999:19).

It is in this context of poverty and inequality within a wealth and job-creating market economy, that we must consider the increasing interest in the school-family-community field in the US and, to a lesser extent, in the UK. As we shall show, a strong rationale for school-family-community initiatives within the US is the hope that they can contribute to the redemption of a dynamic but badly damaged society.

How we undertook the work

For the French and Swedish case studies, we commissioned review papers from Professor Claire Leconte of the University of Lille, and her colleagues Paul and Sophie Craddock, and from Lisbeth Flising at the University of Göteburg. These experts have also acted as respondents to our further queries, and reviewers of our first drafts.

---

2 Table 1 also shows little difference in the average per capita GDP of France, Sweden and the UK, with all three countries substantially lower than the US. Analysis by the EU however confirms varying levels of income inequality behind these averages: Sweden and France are among the four EU member states with the lowest levels of income inequality, while the UK is among the four member states with the highest levels of inequality (Eurostat, 1999: 63)

Our initial trawl through English language databases using keywords like 'school', 'family' and 'community', raised the prospect of thousands of relevant and recent US references. We therefore approached Dr Michelle Seligson, Director of the National Institute for Out-of School Time, at Wellesley College, Massachusetts, who supplied us with many key references, and commented on a draft. Our electronic search continued, using programme initiatives as keywords, and we tracked influential papers cited in the papers we had already obtained. Two sites on the Internet – Laboratory for Student Success and The Future of Children – allowed downloading of up-to-date publications.

While the terms of the UK debate (school inclusion, relations between school, family and community) seemed to resonate in the literature from the US, this was less so in France and Sweden. In other words, it is not clear that these countries recognise and share the same agenda and discourses as the UK and the US. However (see below) we see this less as a problem and more as a means of helping critical thinking about the UK situation.

Why bother?

One final matter remains by way of introduction. Why undertake a cross-national exercise of this kind? Why compare what is happening in France, Sweden and the US? Two answers are of particular relevance to this work. The first is commonly offered in terms such as exchanging experience, transfer of technology, looking for successful programmes or models of good practice and so on. Hearing the experience of other countries can be inspiring, illuminating and thought provoking. But this answer must be treated with caution. Issues of

language, concepts, context and so on require that experiences always be interpreted in relation to the particular setting where they have occurred. The feasibility of transfer or generalisation to another setting must be questioned. We hope that the case study approach which we have adopted will alert the reader to this issue.

The second answer is less often offered, yet in our view is equally if not more important than the first. It concerns the role of cross-national work in assisting a critical understanding of local policies and services. In a recent paper on children's services (Moss and Petrie, 1997), we argued that these services need to be understood in relation to dominant discourses in society and the constructions of childhood that these discourses produce. In doing so, we were drawing on several important fields of work, including the study of discourses and their productive effects (in particular by Michel Foucault), and the burgeoning area of childhood studies and the increasing importance attached to the socially constructed nature of childhood and its institutions (cf. Dahlberg, Moss and Pence, 1999; James and Prout, 1997; James, Prout and Jenks, 1998).

Viewed from this perspective, cross-national work offers the opportunity to view one's own society and its systems through a different lens – in these cases, lenses of American, French or Swedish origin. Through doing so we may become more aware of taken-for-granted assumptions, conceptions, values and power relations that shape thinking and action, and which are embedded in dominant discourses and constructions. This may provide a jolt, because it makes the invisible visible and thereby subject to problematisation, while at the same time making us aware of social phenomena and constructions which are absent from our own society. Cross-national analyses should present critical questions which go beyond how to do things to why to do things, to consider who we think children are and what we think are the purposes of institutions for children. They should broaden issues of management and measurement to become, also, issues of value and ethics.

We are very grateful for the opportunity which the Joseph Rowntree Foundation has given us to pass beyond what Cherryholmes (1988) refers to as a vulgar pragmatism, narrowly concerned with what works, to a critical pragmatism which also questions meanings, assumptions and discourses. It is in this context that we devote space in each of the three national accounts to the discourses that appear to us to be dominant in each country and which produce particular constructions of childhood and shape particular policies and services for children, families and communities.

How the report is organised

This report takes France, the US and Sweden as three national cases, selected because they differ significantly on the parameters outlined above, providing not only interesting experiences but also different perspectives for looking at and questioning our own situation in the UK. For each country, we look at the structure and purposes of the education system, as well as recent policy developments in education and school-family-community relationships. In the chapters on France and Sweden, different aspects of policy are followed directly by accounts of their evaluation. For the US, with a much larger evaluation literature, evaluation is taken as a separate subject.

We considered organising the report around themes, but decided that this would negate the case study approach which attempts to explore the links between policies and practices, and to relate them to the dominant discourses and other aspects of the particular context of each country. However, we end each chapter by summarising key themes that emerge from the case study of that country, while the concluding chapter offers a range of issues and questions that emerge from consideration of the similarities and differences among the three countries.

2 France

Education and schools: structure and purpose

Schooling is organised in four phases: the *école maternelle* (nursery school) for children aged 2 to 6 years (attended by half of 2-year-olds and nearly all 3 to 6-year-olds); compulsory education begins at age 6 in the *école primaire* (primary school), continuing with the *collège* (11 to 14 years) and the *lycée* (15 to 16 years, the end of compulsory education, with most students continuing to 18 years). A 5-year-old child can expect, on average, 16 further years of schooling (OECD, 1997a: Table C1.2). Eighty per cent of students are educated in the state sector with the rest mainly attending state-funded Catholic schools which share the timetables and curricula of the state sector.

Children attend school for 36 weeks per year, with 26 hours of lessons per week at the *école maternelle* and *école primaire* and from 27 to 33 hours, according to age, at the *collège* and with wider variations at the *lycée*. There are no lessons on Wednesday or Saturday afternoons, although there is a trend towards a full day on Wednesday and closure all day Saturday.

Many schools include provision for child care and leisure activities – *services périscolaires*. There are also widespread, and mostly state funded, *services extrascolaires* or out-of-school services.

Staffing in schools primarily consists of teachers (*professeurs des écoles*). In addition, classes in *écoles maternelles* usually include (at least for a half day) an assistant (*agent spécialisé des écoles maternelles*). The training to qualify teachers to work with children from 2 to 11 years was reformed and upgraded in 1991: it now takes five years – a three-year university degree course leading to a *licence* followed by two years' professional training at an *institut universitaire de formation des maîtres* (IUFM). Adults taking part in non-curricular activities (for example, *services périscolaires* and *services extrascolaires*) include parent volunteers, sports staff, artists and class teachers. There are also *animateurs*, non-teaching staff who animate or stimulate children's activities. They are not professionalised, but some are employed for substantial hours and there is non-obligatory training over 30 months, the BAFA. The BAFA comprises an initial eight-day course, 14 days in a practice placement, and a further six to eight days for deepening the candidate's general understanding and enhancing specialist skills.

There is a consensus that the main objectives of education are: 'the transmission of knowledge and general culture, the development of the individual (both for his or her own benefit and as a citizen of France) and preparation for working life' (OECD, 1997c). Republican values of citizenship, equality and secularity are central to French education. One legacy of the republican tradition has been the centralised control of resources and the curriculum, in order to ensure equity. Thus central government recruits and pays staff, formulates the national curriculum and controls the ethos of teaching and learning in schools. However, recent years have seen some movement towards decentralisation in order to meet more local needs. Also stemming from republicanism is the exclusion of the Roman Catholic Church from state schools and, perhaps, an associated reluctance to collaborate with other external agencies (Chambon and Proux, 1993).

Recent developments in French education

Measures such as the reduction of class sizes have contributed to increased educational attainment with the proportion passing the Baccalaureate growing from 25 per cent (around 1980) to 63 per cent (1995) and participation in higher education increasing among all social groups. The educational achievement of the children of immigrants is described as 'fairly satisfactory' (Leconte, Craddock and Craddock) in that differences between them and other students decrease as they move through the system.

There remain major problems, as Leconte and her colleagues observe: 'truancy for Years 7 – 10 and Years 11 – 13 has reached worrying proportions and seems to reflect a general malaise rather than being the result of difficult social conditions ... '

Priority Education Zones (ZEPs)

From 1982, a response to the influence of social background on school performance has been to establish *zones d'éducation prioritaires* (ZEPs). ZEPs reach out to parents and other partners to promote educational achievement in areas where social conditions constitute an obstacle to children's education. Nationally, ZEPs cater for 11 per cent of pupils in state education with variation between areas from 15 per cent of pupils (mostly in urban areas) to less than 5 per cent. In 1999, the Ministry of National Education announced the creation of a thousand new sites classified as ZEPs. ZEPs operate in different ways, for example by health workers visiting families at home, through parental education and support groups, and the appointment of liaison workers for parents for whom French is an additional language. A major objective of ZEPs is to increase the number of 2-year-olds in nursery education. The ZEP policy is seen as largely successful – it was found that ZEPs which succeed are those which achieve real partnerships and aim to become educational communities. This depends essentially on the willingness (not universal) of teachers and head teachers to trust local partners.

School-family-community: recent developments

Decentralisation, cooperation and local partnerships

Laws decentralising education were passed in 1982 and 1985, resulting in a movement from a highly centralised educational system to one which places some decision making and administration with local authorities and the local community and its representatives. The development of educational councils at various levels may also be seen in this context (see below).

The partial decentralisation of education forms part of the background to a growing emphasis on opening schools to local and closer partnerships. Cooperation between schools and museums has existed since before the Second World War (Coppey, 1993). Developments from the 1970s led, in 1988, to the Ministry of National Education and the Ministry of Culture cofinancing cultural and arts workshops. Stronger ties between the Ministries of Culture and of National Education have enabled, for example, the creation of a Baccalaureate in Drama (Lallias 1993). Training Centres for Musicians in Schools, created in the 1990s, aim to give children of all ages an introduction to music during school time. Pupils in Years 7 to 10 are offered courses in art, languages or sport, which can be set up in collaboration with partners. The school timetable can be adjusted for students to receive specialised music teaching at the regional Conservatoire, for example. Leconte and her colleagues note that such classes are becoming increasingly selective and that schools tend to make use of external expertise and resources rather than forming true partnerships with others (see also Best, 1993). Consequently, these relationships do not necessarily make the school more inclusive or open.

Children's use of local resources

Social and educational integration is promoted by citizenship studies, from the *école maternelle* onwards. Allied to citizenship is an emphasis on culture. Publicly-funded care and leisure facilities outside school hours, including residential holiday opportunities for children, are seen as providing for children's education in citizenship and culture as much as a means of child care. Central government money has been provided for local partnerships between schools and local agencies to facilitate children's access to cultural resources and thus their entry into civic life. This follows series of enabling legislation and large-scale pilot schemes. Finance and other support come from ministries, local authorities, voluntary organisations, the *caisses d'allocations familiales* (regional funds providing cash benefits to families and subsidies to services, funded by employers' contributions), the FAS (*Fonds d'action sociale* – the social action fund for immigrant workers and their families) and elsewhere.

The ministries primarily involved have included the Ministry of Youth and Sport (*Ministère de la Jeunesse et des Sports*) and the Minstry of Culture and Education (*Ministère de la Culture et de l'Education*); the actions of other ministries towards children are coordinated at local level (Ministère de la jeunesse et des sports, 1992).

Children's rhythms and reorganising the school week

A specific concern of French psychological research and educational policy has been the circadian or daily psychological and physiological rhythms of the child. This relates to a European concern dating from the outset of compulsory education as to the optimum length and organisation of school hours (Meijvogel, 1991) and builds on French experiments in the 1950s and 1960s (ibid). This concern continues to be emphasised in recent legislation and pilot schemes where it is often coupled with the facilitation of partnerships with agencies outside the school.

School authorities are urged to keep in mind children's daily physical and psychological rhythms. A government circular (Ministère de l'Education National de la Jeunesse et des Sports, 1988) explains that in the early afternoon children are lethargic, so that intellectual activities or intense physical effort are not appropriate. Schools are, therefore, permitted to arrange their hours and activities, curricular and extra curricular, accordingly. During the early afternoon, they may incorporate extra-curricular sport, creative activities and free play, and bring in non-teaching staff (the *service périscolaire* referred to earlier) or take children out to civic amenities and places of interest. More formal class activities then resume, beyond what was previously the end of the school day. After lessons, children are cared for and have recreation until parents collect them.

The policy has been promoted through various government initiatives. By 1990–91, 2,579 schools had reorganised the lunch break, and similar numbers had rearranged the teaching time at the beginning of the afternoon. In the same year, 1,485 schools had integrated early-morning child care, previously separate, into their activities (in 1989–90, no schools had done so). This expansion continues (Leseve-Nicolle, 1994). (See Figure 2.1 for a specimen timetable for a reorganised school week).

An evaluation of this policy of reorganising the school week found positive outcomes for the children, in terms of improved behaviour, greater tolerance in their dealings with others, an improvement in the general climate of the school, less violence and greater participation and concentration in class. It also found positive results for the school, the relationships within it and its openness to the local community. Negative findings included: difficulties in developing school timetables, the tendency to add on activities rather than properly managing the time available and, sometimes, little communication between local organisations and the school (Leseve-Nicolle, 1994).

In 1996, a Ministry of Youth and Sport pilot initiative extended earlier experiments by addressing partnerships in education more fully and involving parents, children, teachers, local councillors and researchers. It also reorganised the school timetable by closing schools on Saturday and curtailing holidays to compensate for this and for the time spent in non-curricular activities during the school day. The initiative seeks both to respect children's circadian rhythms and to provide all children with an introduction to sporting and cultural activities which they may continue in local clubs and associations (Ministère de la Jeunesse et des Sports, 1996).

Professor Leconte's research team at the

Figure 2 – Weekly timetable, Ecole élémentaire, Gutenberg, Strasbourg, France

Timetable	Mon	Tues	Wed	Thu	Fri	Sat
8.15	Class time	Class time	Class time	Class time	Class time	Free time
12.15	Lunch	Lunch	Lunch	Lunch	Lunch	
14.00	Sporting or cultural activities or recreation	Sporting or cultural activities or recreation	Free time	Sporting or cultural activities or recreation	Sporting or cultural activities or recreation	
15.00	Class time			Class time		
17.00						

Translated from the report *Aménagement des Rythmes Scolaires*, Ministère de la Jeunesse et des Sports, 27 August 1996

(At 17.00 classes and other activities end but there is often childcare after that time, as there is before the commencement of lessons in the early morning. Childcare and recreational services are also widely available on Wednesday afternoons and during school holidays, often under the auspices of voluntary organisations.)

University of Lille has been commissioned by the Ministry to evaluate these experiments at several sites throughout the country. Preliminary findings show that local partnerships may be difficult to establish because schools have traditionally limited the participation of outside agencies to input into activities run by teachers, rather than true collaborations. For example, Hocquard (1993) shows that while teachers acknowledge some of their own limitations, with regard to partnerships with industry 'they do not want what they teach or the way they teach to be changed'.

Educational activities in new out-of-school centres

Alongside efforts to bring partners into education, there is also some movement within outside organisations to bring education into their activities. In many districts situated within ZEPs, reception centres have been set up to cater for children outside school hours. This development has not resulted from any initiative by schools or government. Most projects can be traced back to a request from parents. Unlike associations and youth movements, which cater for children's leisure activities outside school hours, the principal aim of these new structures is to help the children with their school work. Although, often, they began with voluntary helpers, these groups now have paid staff and, depending on the local situation, one adult will supervise from five to ten children.

Issues

Parental participation

At a formal level, parental participation in children's education at school has been limited to:

• The participation of parental representatives in

class and school councils, in the CDEN (a council at the level of the *Département*), and in a national Higher Council for Education (CSE). Parents have the right to take time off work to attend these.

• The right to be informed about their child's progress and career path. This is conducted through individual and group meetings, through reports three times per year, and through a diary or notebook, passed between home and school, which details the child's progress and any problems.

• Supporting children's study and learning at home.

By and large, commentators are somewhat negative about the level and quality of parental participation. For example, they point out that parents are not to be found in classrooms, although they are expected to support children's study at home. Leconte and her colleagues comment on the difficulty which outsiders, including researchers, generally meet in attempting to gain access to the classroom.

In contrast, Combes (1998) describes developments within the ACEPP (*Association des Collectifs Enfant Parents*), a publicly-funded grassroots parents association which provides some 13,000 early years services. She compares ACEPP's success, including community development in disadvantaged neighbourhoods, with the traditional exclusion of parents from decision making in schools: 'Most teachers seem to think that, although parents may be useful to accompany field trips, they definitely do not have a necessary and desirable contribution to make to the education process itself.'

Centralisation and decentralisation

The ebb and flow between centralisation and

decentralisation affects the pilot schemes described above. The Ministry of National Education has, since 1998, expressed the desire to regain control of the organisation of the school timetable. Leconte, Craddock and Craddock comment that the Ministry of National Education, the Ministry of Youth and Sport and the Ministry of Culture more often 'see themselves as opponents rather than as being complementary in a common mission: that of educating the child to be a future citizen.' In other words, partnership must be at the level of ministries as well as further down the educational chain.

Conclusion: discourses and constructions

The case of France is complex. Historically, education has been seen as the responsibility of the state and of professionals, with clear purposes that relate to the identity and cohesion of the nation state. The logic of this position has been, and to some extent continues to be, that children, parents and the wider community have little direct part to play in education beyond providing assistance. Nevertheless, there are many public policy initiatives which open the school to the wider community, including parents, and which seek to open up the community to children. The creative vigour of recent legislation and pilot schemes is impressive, especially where the school week and the school year has been reorganised, with the cooperation of teachers, for the sake of children's wellbeing.

There is some evidence that these initiatives are imperfectly realised. Nevertheless, throughout the discourse which informs them is found a strong theme which relates to citizenship and its promotion. It is to be seen underpinning the changing orientation of the state to the school, and the school to the community. There is, firstly, a desired integration of the child as citizen with the larger community, an integration mediated by the school. Secondly, policy must also be seen within the context of decentralisation, with more decision making within the local community, rather than by central government. Thirdly, public policy provides central government money for partnerships that facilitate children's use of local resources, and thus their current entry into civic life (the form this takes is often an explicit contract between various partners for particular types of local development which, once agreed, enables the partnership to receive state funding).

The construction given to the French child is as a future adult citizen of France, who will, through effective education and induction into French culture, be the equal of their peers. A focus on school achievement promotes future equality and secures the child's future civic status. At the same time, more recent policy developments also relate to the child here and now both as a member of the local society, with access to its resources, and as a physiological and psychological person whose daily rhythms need to be recognised and accommodated by the school.

Key themes and features

- extensive system of publicly-funded nursery schooling, child care and leisure services for children of school age
- education is strongly influenced by republican values of citizenship, equality and secularity
- tradition of centralised control of education with some recent moves to greater decentralisation
- improving educational standards prioritised, with strategy of priority education zones to promote equality in education
- social inclusion also promoted by emphasis on citizenship and culture – with education as a means of inducting the child into French citizenship and culture
- growing emphasis on partnerships between schools and other organisations, but schools have difficulties opening up to others, including parents
- different ministries find collaboration difficult
- outside school: development of parent-initiated study support centres and many early years services
- increasing policy and research interest in daily rhythms of the child, expressed in reorganisation of school day, incorporating sport, creative activities and free play

3 The United States

Education and schools: structure and purpose

The patterns of schooling vary, somewhat, by state. Kindergarten, for 4 and 5-year-olds, is mainly school-based and increasingly viewed as the start of universal education, with nearly all children (91 per cent in 1991) attending for some period prior to entering the first grade at age 5 or 6 years. On average children entering at 5 can expect 16 years of schooling, the first 12 of which are compulsory (OECD, 1997a: Table C1.2). Schooling consists of *elementary school* and *high school*, often organised into six years at elementary school (to 12) followed by three years each at junior and senior high schools; other patterns include for example 6-2-4 or 8-4 years (Cincotta et al., 1986). The vast majority of students attend public schools, which are secular, with most others in church-sponsored parochial schools.

The Constitution remains silent on the role of national government in education, and responsibility is devolved to the state and local community. Laws and policy are formulated at state level; locally, schools are operated by more than 15,000 school districts, which are school authorities usually run by elected boards. But from the Kennedy administration (early 1960s) onwards, however, federal involvement in education has increased, focusing on providing encouragement, financial support and leadership. The primary federal responsibility has resided with the Department of Education since it was constituted in 1979.

Three purposes of education in the public school tradition are particularly relevant to this report. First, community building: 'On the 19th century frontier, the school along with the church and jail was a key public building in the community.' (Cincotta et al., 1986: 7). Second, nation building: schools have acted as Americanising agents for immigrants (Cincotta et al., 1986). Third, and closely linked to the first two purposes, public schools have been agents of social change, both to tackle problems and realise visions for the future.

Improving the lot of poor children has long been an objective of the American public school system, with social reformers advocating 'schools as the coordinating organisation that could orchestrate community services and remedy a wide range of social ills' (Wang, Haertel and Walberg, 1998: 2). Kagan (1997) describes schools in the 1890s depression taking on a range of services such as providing meals, kindergartens, health, home visiting, summer programmes and so on. Boyd (1998a) notes that 'the tendency to see the schools as vehicles for the resolution or at least amelioration of social problems is deeply embedded in the public's mind' (7). Popkewitiz (1998) talks of a 'culture of redemption', that is to save and rescue the child and society, a culture which has been embodied by social and educational sciences in America since the 19th century.

Recent developments in American education

Hertert (1996) identifies three waves of educational reform since the early 1980s. The first involved a 'top down' prescriptive control of public education. The second focused on restructuring organisational and governance systems through teacher professionalisation, school-based management and parent involvement. The third wave, inscribed in the 1994 Goals 2000: Educate America Act, emphasises 'systemic reform'. Systemic reform reflects a prevailing analysis of the failure of earlier educational reform on the grounds of inadequate coherence and integration across educational policies. The new approach offers organisation around a set of clear pupil outcomes, combined with greater decentralisation to, and flexibility for, schools which will be held accountable through standardised testing regimes. Thus the current reform wave combines decentralisation with increasing control, more flexibility with increased uniformity reflected in national goals, and a shift from input-driven to outcome-based management (Boyd, 1998b; Hertert, 1996; OECD, 1997b). This is a 'surprising and totally unprecedented development given the strong US tradition of local control of education' (Boyd, 1998b: 3), producing a 'realignment of power, authority and responsibility to provide a policy structure that supports and encourages coherence' (Hertert 1996: 381). It is driven by concerns about meeting the educational needs of the workforce to ensure America's success in an increasingly competitive global economy. The reform is the product of political bipartisanship beginning in 1986, but under strain since the 1994 Congressional elections which brought the ascendancy of right-wing Republicans (Boyd, 1998b). It also involves close collaboration between federal and state levels (OECD, 1997b).

School-family-community: recent developments

Policy

There is a long history of American schools having a wider community role and carrying out a social agenda. By the 1930s, community schools had taken root, rising to full prominence in the 1950s. A commitment to 'expanding the definition and

services associated with schools was reaffirmed in the 1960s, when educational reformers focused on supporting families, not simply the children in them' (Kagan, 1993: 283). While the function of schooling within the global marketplace received increasing emphasis by 1986 teachers accounted for only 52 per cent of all school employees 'indicating that schools had become multipurpose institutions that looked beyond the academic performance of their students' (Wang et al., 1998: 2).

Recently, the relationship between schools, families and community has been prioritised, with parental involvement seen as a necessary condition of successful schooling. In 1994, the eighth national educational goal was set: 'that every school will promote partnerships that will increase involvement and participation in promoting the social, emotional and academic growth of children' (OECD, 1997b: 185). This goal implies that every state will develop policies to assist schools to establish partnerships. These should include parents and involve academic matters and sharing educational decision-making. However, there is no legally binding way in which states can be required to follow this policy (OECD, 1997b). The Federal government can only encourage, support and stimulate partnerships by actions which 'generally focus on freeing schools from regulations and other restrictions so they may locally determine how to design school-community collaboration' (Honig and Jehl, 1999: 22).

Other measures involve funding. Recent national laws, such as Title 1 of the Elementary and Secondary Education Act, support school-family-community partnerships, and target children from low-income families. A Comprehensive School Reform Demonstration Initiative focuses on basic education and parental involvement and assists public schools throughout the country to implement comprehensive school reform based on research and effective practice. The 21st Century Community Center Learning Programme awards grants 'to rural and inner-city public schools or consortia of schools to promote family-community-school cooperation to enable them to plan, implement or expand projects that benefit the educational, health, social services, cultural and recreational needs of the community' (Manning and Rodriguez, 1999: 3). Two hundred million dollars has been awarded under this programme in 1998 and 1999 to around 900 schools in 300 communities, to support activities such as longer opening hours, safe places to do homework, mentoring in basic skills, drug and violence prevention counselling, recreational activities and technology education. Thus the Federal Department of Education has used its influence and resources 'to encourage school-community partnerships and to otherwise steer the use of discretionary grants, waiver provisions and categorical funds for a variety of purposes' (Honig and Jehl, 1999: 21).

Rationale

Four inter-related reasons – educational, social, organisational and recreational – drive this renewed interest in school, family and community partnerships. First, parental involvement in their children's education is considered to contribute to **educational success**, particularly for more disadvantaged children. This leads to the second reason: better **meeting the needs of 'high risk' children and families**. The debate about school-family-community in the US is played out against a backdrop of deep concern about the condition of children and families: poverty, youth crime, children and youth at risk of abuse and neglect,

poor health, unstable families, a 'socially toxic environment' – the litany of problems seems endless and is taken up by many authors who frequently talk of a deteriorating situation (see, for example, Boyd, 1998a; Kagan, 1997; Koppich and Kirst, 1993; Manning and Rodriguez, 1999; OECD, 1997b; Payzant, 1992; Wynn, Meyer and Richards-Schuster, 1999): 'these worsening family and community conditions have stimulated much of the current interest by educators and policy-makers in family, community and school collaboration as one way of responding to what many see as a social and economic crisis' (OECD, 1997b: 184). Many argue that education will not prove successful for 'high risk' children unless it is possible to 'address non-educational problems, usually associated with poverty, that act as barriers to student learning' (Warren, 1999: 1); and that schools have an important role to play in addressing, more generally, the social crisis affecting so many children, families and communities.

The third reason concerns **the need to rethink the organisation and delivery of services for children and families**. Established ways of doing things are perceived to be failing: 'the traditional fragmentation of responsibility among a variety of agencies for a large array of social and health services needed by poor children and families are increasingly viewed as dysfunctional and unacceptable' (Boyd, 1998a: 10). Increasingly schools are seen as a logical access point, indeed often the only functioning access point, in many neighbourhoods and communities (Merseth et al., 1999). Moreover, schools are currently often underused, parents and children know where they are located and they are usually considered safe (DeWitt Wallace-Reader's Digest Fund (1999)). More positively, there is a search for a transformed understanding and organisation of services, creating 'an integrated care and education system which includes a dramatic reconceptualisation and restructuring of relations between the school, the community and the larger society' (Boyd, 1999a: 11)

The fourth reason is **'to provide an array of positive activities for young people during nonschool hours'** (Dewitt Wallace-Reader's Digest Fund, 1999: 1). This is partly about enhancing educational achievement and personal development, since 'young people attending formal after-school programs spend more time in academic activities and in enrichment lessons than do their peers left unsupervised after school' (US Department of Education, 1998: 13). But it is also about preventing juvenile delinquency, vandalism and other antisocial behaviour – 'keeping children on the right track' – through schools providing activities for young people outside school hours to replace activities that are regarded as of little value (such as 'hanging out') or as leading to harm. Overall, the most cited purpose of these programmes is providing adult supervision of children (Seppanen et al, 1993), in the context of an increasingly dangerous environment, increasing parental employment and the evidence that many 5 to 14-year-olds (about 1.6 million in 1991) are unsupervised while their parents are at work (Casper, Hawkins and O'Connell, 1994).

Although presented as separate rationales, these represent a clutch of connected public concerns about the performance of schools, educational standards and what is happening to and in families and neighbourhoods – all of which spread beyond 'at risk' children. One response is to look to the school to provide a more inclusive approach – to offer new hope of redemption, stability and community.

Service development

A new and unprecedented wave of school-community initiatives has appeared over the last decade and grown exponentially (Kagan, 1997; Mclaville and Blank, 1999). As 'schools have become the location of choice for collaborative programmes' (Wang et al., 1998: 3), there is widespread development of school-linked health and human services programmes. These provide assistance to children and youth in high-risk settings and 'reach out to families beset by urgent problems including poverty, teenage pregnancy, single parenthood, substance abuse, limited health care and inadequate and unaffordable housing' (Wang et al., 1998). They have various titles: school-linked services, community schools, extended-services schools or full-service (community) schools.

Nearly all school-linked programmes develop 'mechanisms for effective communication, coordinated service delivery and mobilization of community resources' (ibid.: 2), but with no single model. Instead, collaborative programmes

> vary in the composition and intensity of services delivered, skill of staff and mode of delivery, and target group served. They range from single, one component partnerships between a school and an outside agency or business to sophisticated, complex, multi-component, multi-agency collaborations. In most cases, services are joined to the schools via informal agreements, contractual agreements, established systems of referral and sometimes mechanisms that enable staff members of various community agencies to be outposted or shared ... variations also exist in the type of collaboration practised. While

most centres have moved beyond simple cooperation towards more coordinated activity (i.e. defined by degree of institutional autonomy of the partners), they differ in the negotiated order among participating agencies (Boyd, 1998a: 11–12).

School-linked programmes vary along a number of parameters:

- physical **locations** of collaborative services (Driscoll et al., 1998), including school campuses and off-campus sites. In their study of 20 initiatives, Melaville and Blank (1999) report that the bulk of activities take place in school grounds, but most also use – at least occasionally – community locations such as churches, housing complexes and neighbourhood centres.

- **times of the day** when available. Every initiative studied by Melaville and Blank (1999) provided after-school activities, which, in about two-thirds of cases, continued into the evening; less than half operated before school or at weekends.

- **governance and day-to-day management.** Melaville and Blank (1999) report that 'primary oversight' was largely community-based, but day-to-day management was much more school centred.

- **organisations involved**, including health and social service agencies, community-based organisations, businesses and government agencies.

- **services provided**. There is variation in the number and breadth of services offered, from a single service to attempts to provide fully comprehensive services (Wynn et al., 1999). Services include: child care centres, school-age child care, health services (such as clinics), social services (for example, family support groups, child protection, probation, parenting education), academic remediation and support (for example, adult education and literacy, tutoring, mentoring, homework help), vocational competency (such as training in pre-employment skills, career development counselling, job training, vocational education), and basic subsistence (food, clothing and housing and legal assistance). Melaville and Blank found that tutoring and literacy, parent education, school-age child care, leadership development and employment and job training were 'the five most salient areas of activity across the field' (15). In their survey of 137 programmes, Driscoll et al. (1998) found an average of 14 services per programme, with 'parenting education' the most common (81 per cent), followed by 'family support and advocacy' (69 per cent) and 'other health education' (67 per cent); only a third provided adult education and literacy or employment-related services.

- **kinds of personnel** working in school-community initiatives, 'ranging from nurse practitioners, substance abuse counsellors, volunteer senior citizens, case managers and community policy, to clergy' (Dryfoos, 1994: 4).

- **origins** (for example, public sector, private sector, traditional service delivery organisations, grassroots community organisations) and **partners** (for example, schools, families, social and health care workers, as well as, to a lesser extent, universities, private foundations, religious institutions, law enforcement, business).

- **concerns, perspectives and goals** also vary, including 'improved educational quality and academic outcomes for young people (School Reform); more efficient and effective health and social services delivery to meet the comprehensive needs of children and families (Services Reforms); increased recognition of the developmental needs of young people ... (Youth Development); and expanded efforts to strengthen the human, social and economic underpinnings of neighbourhoods and communities (Community Development)' (Melaville and Blank, 1999: 5).

- **relationships between services**. Adelman and Taylor (1997) suggest five possibilities – informal, coordinated, partnerships, collaborations and integrated services – which differ in the amount of system change needed, and the means of supporting collaboration (for example, using site coordinators and case managers).

- **participants**, including students and their families and, less often, other community residents (Wynn et al., 1999).

The two most recognised models of school-linked services (Boyd, 1998a) are Zigler's *Schools for the 21st Century* (Zigler and Lang, 1991) – which links family support and child care systems – and Comer's (1985) *School Development Program* – which places heavy emphasis on mental health services, and the strengthening and redefining of relationships between school staff, parents and students. A Coalition for Community Schools brings together 125 diverse organisations to promote community schools across the US, based on five key principles: quality education, youth development, family involvement, community development and family support (Merseth et al., 1999). Dryfoos (1994), one of the leaders of this movement, suggests that at least 16,000 full-service schools should be developed, particularly in the 20 per cent of US schools where half or more of students are eligible for free lunches. She also envisages 'full-service community schools' with a school principal and programme coordinator working as peers to provide a seamless one-stop environment, supportive of children and delivering the education, health, social and cultural services required in the community (Dryfoos, 1998).

Evaluation

Despite the high profile given to these initiatives, there is no comprehensive and exact information on their number and type (Driscoll et al., 1998). In 1993–94, about 30 per cent of public schools and 48 per cent of private schools offered extended-day programmes, a substantial increase on the 16 per cent and 33 per cent of six years earlier; 11 per cent of pupils attended public schools with such programmes, compared with 18 per cent in private schools (National Center for Educational Statistics, 1997). However, it is not stated how many of these programmes form part of larger school-family-community initiatives, rather than offering only after-school care. An OECD report (1997b) acknowledges 'a great variety of innovative experiments ... in the area of parental involvement in schools', yet counsels caution:

> [P]erhaps one in ten US schools has moved beyond a few traditional ways of involving parents and families ... [T]here are few comprehensive programmes in place, and in most schools, current practises are episodic

and highly dependent on the presence of funding (195).

Programmes are mostly located in elementary and junior high schools, raising the issue of engaging older students (Melaville and Brown, 1999). They are found mainly in communities and schools with the greatest need, and are used most by the highest risk students (Dryfoos, 1994; Wang et al., 1998; Warren, 1999; Wynn et al., 1999).

The actual level of organisational change involved is not as radical as much of the rhetoric would suggest (Dryfoos, 1994). While services may be partially located within the school, the agencies responsible for them are not involved in the school restructuring or its governance. Adelman and Taylor (1997) likewise note that 'true integration involves blending resources and shared governance, while the current state is mostly about collaboration' (412).

Processes

The evaluation literature to date can throw more light on process than outcomes. It can prove hard to institutionalise collaborations, and unless led by strong champions of coordination, schools tend to continue business as usual (Boyd, 1998a). Kagan (1997) concludes that the process of establishing support systems is 'often laborious, somewhat imprecisely conceived and subject to contextual variables often beyond the control of programme planners' (287). Boyd (1998a) offers some emerging principles for inter-agency collaboration, including quality leadership; long-term commitment to programme development; policies and practices that are culturally compatible; stable funding; incorporation into the regular budget; and attention to space and training. Melaville and Blank (1999)

emphasise the importance of the 'quality of on-site coordination', and the necessity for a full-time coordinator. Their recommendations include: intensified involvement of the private sector and development of community-based collaborative bodies; expanded public sector leadership; site selection and expansion plans around school clusters that include the full range of schools to ensure coverage for all age groups (see also Warren, 1999); using community-based locations more, especially for weekends; and improved technical assistance, especially to develop results-based accountability systems.

There is a need for better information on process, including 'linkage between agencies, the changing role of administrators in schools and service agencies as they collaborate, the changing role of staff and the establishment of management information systems' (ibid., 12). Evaluating collaboration is difficult, not least because of issues about what should be measured, for example linkages among institutions, the accessibility of services to clients or the satisfaction of collaborators.

Outcomes

'With regard to outcomes, there is less definitive material' (Kagan, 1997: 287). Many exemplary school-linked programmes are at too early a stage of development for their effectiveness to be assessed (Boyd, 1998a). Evaluations are 'often method flawed, with high attrition rates, control groups that are not comparable with intervention groups, program variation and unspecified or unmeasurable outcomes' (Kagan, 1997: 287). Furthermore, Kagan notes, evaluation is made more difficult because of external factors, including changes in the nature and level of support received. Melaville and Blank, 1998, found it impossible to link specific approaches to specific outcomes, 'partly because most of the initiatives did not yet have sufficient outcome data, but also because the various approaches they examined were evolving and often blended into one another making causal attribution difficult, if not impossible' (Merseth et al., 1999: 17).

Reviewing 44 sources describing one or more collaborative school-based programmes, Wang et al.(1998) concluded that the empirical results were generally encouraging, with 80 per cent of measured outcomes proving positive, but were largely based on evaluations, which often

> contain inadequate descriptions of the program components, use a limited number of outcomes, have few direct measures of collaboration, do not collect process or implementation data, do not have comparable control groups, have high rates of attrition and report little data of program costs (11).

An evaluation of a school-linked service programme in New Jersey found little evidence of academic improvement. The researcher concluded that 'while school-linked programs can help address students non-academic needs, they cannot be expected to have strong educational outcomes unless they also have strong educational components' (Warren, 199: 2). Honig and Jehl (1999) also conclude that research to date does not indicate that responding to the non-academic needs of pupils will lead to improved academic performance. Pupil success requires non-academic support services (health, recreation and so on), but academic results will not improve significantly without schools restructuring to support learning, including rethinking the role of teachers: 'it is not simply enough to remove non-academic barriers to

youths' learning. School-community sites must proactively enable it – they must marshal and/or create the resource, supports and occasions where learning can occur' (6).

At present, there is an abundance of information that can provide clues to effects, rather than definitive answers about them. Most innovative programmes have not yet provided evidence of replicable, long-term effects (Wang et al., 1998) or about costs (Melaville and Blank, 1999). Overall, Wang et al. conclude that the results must be treated with 'guarded optimism' until results from more rigorous evaluations are available; more than a dozen intensive studies are currently underway looking more closely at long-term outcomes. Merseth and her colleagues (1999), however, question whether definitive answers can be produced: 'these complicated, messy, evolving interventions do not yield themselves to randomized experiments that produce definitive conclusions about causation' (18).

Issues

Barriers to partnership
A number of barriers to partnership have been identified, including:

- **Training –** the professionals involved in school-linked services often lack adequate training for their changing roles (Kagan, 1997; Koppich and Kirst, 1993; OECD, 1997).

- **Resources and sustainability –** 'both mortality and mutation are common events' among collaborative services (Driscoll et al., 1998: 6); when short-term funding stops, so too do the activities (OECD, 1997b; Hertert, 1997). Initial financial and political support often wane over time (Kagan, 1997) and continuity of leadership, political or otherwise, is important (Brown and Hara, 1999; Melaville and Blank, 1999). Melaville and Blank (1999) note that school-community initiatives have a history of highs and lows, and ask what the field must do to sustain and 'scale-up' work. Seligson (personal communication) suggests there are two underlying question. Who will pay for schools to expand their boundaries and missions, at a time when many suffer from shrinking education budgets (based on property taxes), and have to cut existing 'extras' like music and art? And, where funding does exist, is there an adequate infrastructure to administer new services?

- **Shortage of time –** given the new roles for professionals, there is a need for 'redeploying time for program coordination, development and leadership' (Adelman and Taylor, 1997: 419). Collaboration takes time as well as money (Adler, 1993; Brown and Hara, 1999; Payzant, 1992); Driscoll et al. (1998) found lack of time to confer was most often reported, while Hertert (1996) reports 'many (local educators) complained that the state did not provide sufficient time to fully explore, plan and evaluate the required changes' (391).

Shortage of time may also affect parents. The 1997 OECD report observes that 'another major impediment to partnership between parents and schools is the fact that parents – including two-thirds of mothers – are often at work ...' and suggests that 'schools and parents could find new ways to ensure involvement if plans and schedules were adjusted to individual needs and interests'. However, given the long, and some

argue increasing, working hours prevalent in the US and the increasing pressures faced by many working parents (Hochschild, 1997), the issue of parents' labour market participation may prove a resistant barrier. Despite the apparent magnitude of what Hochschild calls the 'time bind', the issue figures little in the literature reviewed. Increasing parental employment (and concomitant changes in parents' employment in what Sennett (1998) calls the 'new capitalism') may be at irreconcilable odds with increasing parental involvement in schools.

- **Conflicting interests, perspectives and cultures –** the traditional culture and autonomy of schools can make them one of the more troublesome partners in collaborative efforts (Kagan, 1997), with incoming agencies expected to conform to the school culture (Crowson and Boyd, 1996). Further barriers include: 'absence of a common language with which to work together'; 'turfism' (see, for example, Warren, 1999); confidentiality (Crowson and Boyd, 1996; Payzant, 1992); and eligibility criteria (Payzant, 1992).

Also debated is how far coordination is an issue of individuals or institutions. Adler (1993) argues that '[o]rganizations can constrain or enable inter-organization efforts, but collaboration is a person-to-person activity' (10). Smylie and Crowson (1996) place primary importance on institutions, arguing that 'an organization's behaviour cannot be fully explained in terms of the behaviours of its individual members' (5). Crowson and Boyd (1996) conclude that organizational knowledge is important for collaborative success and that the developing literature on 'new institutionalism' offers important insights.

The role of the school

Some educationists raise a more fundamental issue: whether working on non-academic needs and school-linked services promotes or interferes with education. For example, the Education Trust 'asserts that calls for school people to get more involved in after-school activities and in reforming services and building neighbourhood cohesion will only detract and distract educators from their core academic mission' (Merseth et al., 1999: 14). From this perspective educational outcomes are most likely to improve 'when the school and school district put their highest priority on improving instruction ... (and) non-academic services are best accomplished when community-based organisations and agencies take responsibility for initiating, organizing and sustaining the needed services and supports' (ibid.: 19). The school's contribution to improved services at the school-community intersect should be to put their facilities 'at the disposal of community-based organisations during non-school hours and providing school personnel with the training to enable them to make optimum use of non-academic services and supports'.

Different reform movements

Adelman and Taylor (1997) suggest that two reform movements need to be distinguished and considered separately. First, there is a **movement to restructure community health and human services**, which shows considerable interest in connecting with schools to better address the needs of 'at risk' or disadvantaged children and families (Warren, 1999). Second, there is a **school reform movement, concerned with removing barriers to learning**, and requiring that more attention be paid to education support programmes and services, which are often 'narrowly focused, fragmented and

oriented to discrete problems and not a prominent part of a school's organisational structure and daily functions' (411):

> ... [c]omprehensiveness requires more than outreach to link with community resources, more than coordination of school-owned services and more than community of school and community services. Moving towards comprehensiveness encompasses restructuring and enhancing 1) school-owned programs and services and 2) community resources; in the process, it is essential to 3) weave school and community resources together. The result is not simply a reallocation or relocation of resources; it is a total transformation of the nature and scope of intervention activity (415).

Competitive concerns

Some service providers question the impact on 'the industry of service providers already out there' by making the school a more general provider of services (personal communication, Michelle Seligson). Many small providers, who have been caring for children after school for years, look askance at schools getting into the 'child care business'. They may feel disadvantaged by a government initiative such as the 21st Century Community Learning Centers Program whose funding goes only to schools, and not to community-based organisations (although schools may choose to contract with such organisations).

Concerns are not just around funding, but also standards. These may not arise if the school acts simply as landlord for services run by other agencies. But if there is more involvement by schools, what are their quality standards or controls? How can schools become attuned and responsive to non-academic needs of children and families?

Conclusion: discourses and constructions

American discourses around this area appear similar to those in the UK. There is a strong emphasis on the redemption of poor children and families through the application of scientific, technical and managerial concepts and methods. Not only are businesses sought as partners in projects, but much of the language draws on business values, constructs and methods. The recent OECD report (1997b) notes that 'parents as partners in education are seen in terms of business partners, wherein both sides need to clarify their mutual interests and common benefits' (186). Kagan suggests that reform is part 'of a national *zeitgeist* that seeks to re-examine our way of doing business ... the norm is to be driven by, and understood in terms of, mission and results' (288). The involvement of business is rarely problematised (for an exception, see the account by Mickelson and Wadsworth (1996) of a project which collapsed in the face of local opposition which questioned its business assumptions and corporate involvement – 'their social construction of the origins and purposes of the Odyssey Program reveal activists' keen awareness of class issues embedded in the struggle over school reform' (331)).

The focus in the discourse is on the how, that is, the solutions, much less on the why, the conceptualisation of the problem and the analysis of cause: 'there is little debate about the desired outcomes for children ... (Merseth et al., 1999: 1). Similarly, there is little analysis of how the crisis of children and families – if crisis it is – may have

originated, and the implications of such an analysis for the possibility and direction of effective intervention. Kagan (1997) proposes that 'it is the political economy of the nation, along with the priorities it sets, that influences family functioning' (278), as does Adler (1993). But such statements are not related to a rigorous problematisation of that political economy nor the possibilities for change. One consequence is an apparent contradiction: a rhetoric of equality and social justice together with a recognition that American society adheres to a highly competitive and market-driven capitalism for which equality and social justice are not values.

While much of the discussion is about children, and in particular their poor structural position, there is no discussion about who children might be nor about childhood or the possibility of its social construction (there are, for example, no references to the important and growing body of European literature on childhood). As Baker (1998) observes, in relation to the American public school, 'much educational work flows around assumptions about children and their development – but what is meant by being a 'child' is not debated' (118). It is highly significant that 'children's issues became part of the public policy agenda in large part because of the publication of very alarming statistics about the conditions of children' (Adler, 1993: 5).

The American discourse on childhood has, therefore, embodied an implicit construction of children as victims or perpetrators (cf. the frequently recurring language of 'at risk', 'in need', 'disadvantaged' etc.), as vulnerable and in need of rescue (what Baker (1998) refers to as 'childhood-as-rescue', the new redemptive theme in American discourse on youth), as reproducers of knowledge who must achieve pre-determined standards and as initial empty vessels who need to be made 'ready to learn' by the time they start school. There is an implicitly individualistic approach to children, with no recognition in the discourse that children might be understood as a social group and no reference to concepts such as children's culture or children's rights or indeed to the possibility of children themselves having agency: Kagan refers to 'schools refocusing their efforts on collaborative decision making that accords more power to staff and, in some cases, parents'(287) – but makes no reference to pupils' contribution to decision-making.

In the American discourse, childhood emerges as a state of adulthood in waiting. Children as becoming adults are valued (or feared) for what they will be when 'fully developed' (the discourse of 'development' producing adulthood as a completed state of being): 'because children are the perfect embodiment of the future, (they) figure prominently in both our aspirations and consternations about the future' (Merseth et al.,

1999: 2). Indeed, as already noted much of the rationale of American educational reform is framed in terms of preparing a better-educated workforce to enhance future economic competitiveness. More broadly, with proper interventions, American children can also redeem society and secure its future, the analysis by Hatch (1995) of the late 19th century seeming to ring true a hundred years later:

> [An] emerging reliance on science and technology ... led to the perception that children are appropriate vehicles for solving problems in society. The notion was that if we can somehow intervene in the lives of children, then poverty, racism, crime, drug abuse, and any number of social ills can be erased. Children became instruments of society's need to improve itself, and childhood became a time during which social problems were either solved or determined to be unsolvable (119)

Key themes and features

- strong decentralisation of education to states and school districts, reflected in diversity of policy and practice, but increased federal involvement since 1960s
- strong tradition of schools as agents of social change, tackling problems and contributing to community and nation building
- recent 'systemic' education reform emphasising strong state-federal collaboration; a shift from input-driven to outcome-based management; national education goals
- educational and other anxieties have stimulated a new wave of school-community service developments, mainly in 'high need' schools
- evaluation to date has more to say on process than outcome, with little evidence so far of replicable, long-term effects
- barriers to partnership include training, resources and sustainability, time and conflicting interests and cultures
- US discourses emphasise the redemption of poor children and families; focus on how rather than why and with little discussion of childhood; understand children as vulnerable, in need of rescue, reproducers of knowledge and adults in waiting.

4 Sweden

Education and schooling

The discourses around children and childhood, learning and knowledge, are distinct and powerful in Sweden (see the end of this chapter) and must be taken into account and given full weight if the aspirations of the Swedish educational system are to be understood. What may seem different from a British (and American) perspective, is the importance attached in Sweden to work that is more theoretical and conceptual in nature and how such work informs policy development. As well as interesting solutions, Sweden raises critical questions about childhood, learning and knowledge, among other issues.

Structure

An extensive system of publicly-funded early childhood services provides education and care for children aged 1 to 5 years. Approximately 70 per cent of children in this age group use these services, mostly in centres but also in organised family day care. Services are open from 6.30am to 6.00pm, with most children attending six to eight hours a day. There are also free social and educational services for very young children accompanied by their parents or family day carers.

For 6-year-olds there are free pre-school classes, used by 95 per cent of the age group, available usually for three hours a day. Increasingly these are integrated with the lower grades of compulsory school. By law children must attend school from the age of 7 to 16: schooling itself is free though parents pay for the cooked midday meal that all schools provide. Around 98 per cent of children attend local authority schools, the rest are in 'free schools' or private schools. After compulsory school age, upper secondary schools offer three further years of schooling, academic or vocational, with about 95 per cent of 16 to 19-year-olds attending.

Publicly-funded free-time services (school-age child care) are provided for children aged 6 to 12 years. About 55 per cent of 6 to 9-year-old children attend, and 7 per cent of 10 to 12-year-olds.

Services are usually organised in a centre within the school, with opening hours commonly from 7 am until lessons start, and from the end of the school day until 5 or 6 pm. During holidays these services are usually open the whole day. For 10 to 12-year-olds, there are also 'open-door' activities, which often cooperate with voluntary organisations (mostly sports clubs).

There are three main types of worker: the pre-school teacher (*förskollärare*) in early childhood centres and the free-time pedagogue (*fritidspedagog*) in free-time services, each with a three-year education at university level; and the school teacher, with a three-and-a-half to four-and-a-half years education, also at university level. Pre-school classes, lower grades in compulsory school and free-time services are increasingly integrated. Teachers, pre-school teachers and free-time pedagogues belong to the same union, and increasingly work in teams within the classroom; all may become the school principal or, within some local authorities, take responsibility for clusters of schools and other services for pre-school and school-age children.

Recent developments in Swedish education

Integration of services

Early years services and free time services for school-age children now fall within the education system, alongside schools, and all are viewed as engaged with children's learning. This means that nationally, the policy remit falls to the Ministry of Education, with administrative responsibility in the hands of the National Agency for Education. This, however, is recent: until 1996 early years and free-time services were the responsibility of the Ministry of Social Affairs and the National Board of Health and Social Welfare. The integration of responsibility for these services within education began earlier in the 1990s at local authority level and was widespread by the time national responsibility was integrated. As a result of the change of perspective and administration, new departments have been formed in local authorities to take responsibility for pre-school services, schools and free-time services.

Entitlement to services

These developments have been accompanied by legislation, in 1993, which places a duty on local authorities to provide early childhood and free-time services for children from 1 to 12 years where parents are employed or studying, as well as for children with particular needs.

Curriculum

The development of services has also given rise to developing and coordinating their curricula. A new and short national curriculum for schools (grades 1 to 9) has been written which sets two kinds of goals, goals to reach and goals to strive towards: 'Goals to strive towards indicate the direction of the work of the school ... Goals to reach express what the pupils at least shall have reached when they leave school. It is the responsibility of the school and the school head that the pupils are given the possibility to reach these goals.' (Lpo -94: 10).

The interpretation and realisation of goals is devolved to the local authorities who formulate their own plans, and to the schools, who work to achieve the goals of the national curriculum within the framework set by their local authority.

Since 1998 a national curriculum for pre-school services (for children aged 1 to 5 years) has been in place and the national curriculum for schools has been extended to include pre-school classes (for 6-year-olds) and free-time services. 'The preschool class is a part of the school and the first step towards realizing and fulfilling the goals of the curriculum. Free-time services shall contribute to reaching the goals' (Lpo -98: 2).

Whole day school

The integration of services at the administrative and curriculum levels has also supported the integration of services within schools. Whole day schools which integrate school classes (either first grades of compulsory school on their own or integrated with pre-school classes) with free-time services are increasingly widespread, although there are still variations in the extent of integration as well as content and organisation. They depend on teamwork between different types of staff:

> The idea of team work was evoked as early as the 1970s both in the committee on childcare and in the committee of the inner work of school (SOU 1974:53). Eventually, the school and child care grew nearer to each other and the activities began to cooperate and began, more and more to be integrated ... Could the future team open the school to the outer world? Is cooperation between preschool-school-school age childcare the educational model of the future? ... The existing work within the integrated school makes a way of work possible where more competences are at

children's and young people's disposal (Rohlin, 1997: 90–91).

In a study of 59 field experiments on cooperation and integration between school and free-time services, Björn Flising (1995) found both problems and potential benefits. He concluded that both have basic similarities: they aim to support children's development and contribute to the quality of life, they work with children of the same age, often with the same children, and both have staff with educational training and competence. The main work of school is about teaching and learning 'established knowledge', while free-time pedagogy is directed towards supporting development in a broader sense, giving children space and time, and resources for play, creativity, friendships, their own interests and explorations. Together the different approaches allow children a more holistic development. Crucial matters are: common management (for example, an interested and energetic joint head teacher); advance preparation (one year) for cooperation or integration; combined planning, follow up, evaluation and development; premises which function well for both sets of activities; and support and freedom for staff to develop cooperative work; and, he stresses, a central role for children.

Hansen (1999) has focused on staff from the two different traditions and cultures (teachers and free-time pedagogues). Team work is not without problems and many investigations show difficulties. A three year project on team work development is being conducted by the Association of Local Authorities in Holland, involving about 30 teams, with a report due to be published this year.

School-family-community: recent developments

The School Committee

Since the 1970s there has been a strong trend towards decentralisation in all aspects of Swedish governance, for example, the national School Committee, formed in 1995, 'with instructions to illustrate the inner workings of the public educational system ... and suggest measures to stimulate educational development' (SOU 1997: 121: 1). Interim reports have included: *Parents in self administered schools* (SOU 1995: 103); *Influence for real – About pupils' rights of influence, participation and responsibility* (SOU 1996: 22) and *Crash or meeting – about the multicultural school'* (SOU 1996: 143). The final report – *School matters: About school in a new age* (SOU 1997: 121) – examines public policy for decentralisation, emphasising the role of the local community and of parents:

> We see two lines of development in a decentralized system. On the one hand you have to give support to teachers so that they can broaden their self-governed space and strengthen their self-esteem. On the other hand the local community has to be involved in the inner work of the school. Parents and others outside school ought to participate in discussions about education with their questions, their views, needs and so on. In this there are important developmental possibilities for the school (7)

Supporting parenthood

An official investigation was set up to examine how parents may best be supported regarding children's education. The 1997 report reveals a changed view of relations between family and society. It abandons notions of parental education based on society 'knowing best' with knowledge needing to be transmitted to parents. Instead, parents (like their children) are seen as capable of constructing knowledge themselves, aided by the tools that interaction with other people and life experience can give them. Local networks are still important, as are professionals, but in a different way from before. Parents themselves know if and how they need support. The report argues that 'parent education' is too narrow and recognises the importance of more informal contacts and meetings between parents, or between parents and professionals:

> It can be the 'entrance hall chat' with the preschool teacher in the daycare centre. It can be the 'developmental conversation' together with the child and school staff. It can be conversations with other parents and leaders at the school camp. These are meetings where parents can be given opportunities to air their views and thoughts together with others who have experience and professional knowledge of children and parenthood. It is also about utilizing and developing the networks that exist around many, but far from all, parents. At other times it can be about intimate conversation in private with someone who has special professional knowledge, for example the psychologist at the child welfare clinic or the family therapist at the family guidance ...
> [The aim] is, in short, to give knowledge, information, advice and support in order to develop parents' competence and to

strengthen their security and self-reliance as parents from pregnancy up to and including the whole of their child's adolescence. They ought to be able to develop their own roles as parents based on their own conviction of what a good parent is. (SOU, 1997: 161: 10–11)

At the same time the report recognised that society sometimes needs to seek out and offer special support.

The relationship between school and parents is also covered in the new curriculum (see above) and extends parents' competence:

> The school is then to be a support to the families in their responsibility for the upbringing and development of the children ... Everybody who works in school shall cooperate with the pupils' carers in order to be able to develop educational content and activity together (Lpo-94: 7, 16).

Parents' influence in schools

Lisbeth Flising reports that parents are an important but so far relatively unused resource in the Swedish school. Many investigations have shown that parents want more influence over their children's schooling. For some, influence may mean choosing their child's school, for others participating in planning school activities. Many parents wish to be treated with respect by the staff and to be able to put forward ideas and views that are treated seriously. Others want to discuss educational activities and their rationale. What different parents mean by influence relates to their own situation in society, their work, spare time interests, education and so on – and the same is true of preschool and free-time services.

There is some anxiety, especially from school staff, that if parents get to exert influence they will take over the school activities. Teachers also wonder how they could meet the different wishes of all parents. Research shows that these fears are mostly exaggerated. Most parents say that they want to discuss school activities, to be involved and bring suggestions and ideas (Flising, Fredriksson and Lund 1996).

In its final report, the School Committee discusses the necessary knowledge base for parents' exercise of influence:

> One objection [to more parental influence in the school] was that parents lack competence to participate in decision making concerning the central issues in school. We maintain that parents, in order to take part in school affairs, do not need any other competence than the one they already possess as parents, professionals and citizens ... What parents can supply is above all knowledge about their own children. Furthermore parents can share their experiences from work life, from local society and from the spare time activities of the children. Parents' lack of knowledge about school is a passing phenomenon. By and by they will, through participating in work in school, learn much about school and the conditions of the school (SOU, 1997:121).

Parental influence in schools has increased recently in different ways. First, many schools are now governed by **local boards with parents in the majority**. At present this is for an experimental period of five years. The local boards consist of parents, school staff and always the principal; pupils may also be part of the board. The local authority decides on the board's responsibilities and has ultimate responsibility. Duties which may be devolved from the local authority and the school principal include the timing of the school day; the responsibility to offer pupils a broad selection of subjects; and decisions on the local work plan, the development of competencies for staff, forms of cooperation between school and family, and bullying and harassment policies. Research on the boards provides mainly positive results (see, for example, Ritchey, 1998), although a study of ten schools shows some insecurity and suspicion. On the one hand parents can feel that they become hostages for cuts in services while on the other it may be their only chance to exercise influence on the schools (Kristoffersson, 1998).

Second, the place and underlying values of **developmental conversations** are outlined in the national curriculum. These are meetings between the teacher, the pupil and the parent/s and sometimes the preschool teacher or the free-time pedagogue, replacing the school report and the former 'quarter of an hour' conversations. The developmental conversation should be on an equal level between the three participants, forward looking, using the present situation as a starting point, and well prepared for by, and resulting in mutual commitments from, all three participants.

This developmental conversation has been widely introduced and welcomed. Development work and research is ongoing. Lisbeth Flising (1997) has studied problems about pupils' and parents' preparation for a conversation, and the unequal position of the pupil within the conversation, dependent on and outnumbered by the adults.

Örebro University is conducting a study evaluating the usefulness of a leaflet distributed to parents in all schools *Learn to learn through the portfolio and the developmental conversation.* (The portfolio is a collection of pupils' work covering the whole of their school life and providing a concrete focus, which may facilitate pupils' part in the conversation).

Other developments include: producing material for parents' study groups (*Growing Together*) which are popular from preschool through the whole of compulsory schooling including for immigrant parents; and a project in Malmö about the relation between family, preschool and school and the changing distribution of responsibility during the next century.

Pupils' influence in schools

While at an ideological level it is considered obvious that pupils should influence their own educational activities and situation, in practice the picture is more complex. Much research shows that pupils rarely have real influence in school, especially over education itself. Research by the School Committee (see above) concludes that

> the pupils would like to have influence. Above all they want to be able to influence their daily work situation. In all investigations in which the pupils speak for themselves, they stress the importance of an open and active dialogue between teacher and pupils. We found that pupils' suggestions seldom led to any changes. (op cit.: 104)

The School Committee suggested the establishment of pupil forums, for 'the support of pupils in a broad sense'. The facilitation of networks of forums was also proposed.

Lisbeth Flising reports many developments, including an experiment in Western Sweden to involve pupils in the development of different school subjects and general participation in decision making. In most schools in Sweden there are special anti-bullying groups consisting of both pupils and teachers and sometimes other professionals such as nurses and psychologists. Since 1993 the National Agency for Education has conducted a project on pupil influence which resulted in a book entitled *I want to have influence over everything* (Tham, 1998). This aimed to deepen and broaden the picture of what pupil influence is and could be:

> It is about work in school, ergonomics and other working conditions, formal processes of decision making and management. But pupils' influence also concerns daily work in the classrooms and each pupil's influence over her or his own learning and learning processes.

Children and childhood

Discourses and constructions

Sweden is moving from an industrial society into a post-industrial, information and knowledge society – a learning society. There is also a profound change – a paradigmatic shift – in how people understand and create meaning in their lives which has consequences for understandings of children and childhood. While many teachers retain the view of the child as 'the empty box', with question and answer as their most important pedagogical method an alternative view is becoming increasingly common. This way of viewing the child

builds on the notion of the child as an active

and creative actor, as a subject and citizen with potentials, rights and responsibility. A child worth listening to and having a dialogue with, and who has the courage to think and act by himself ... the child as an active actor, a constructor, in the construction of his own knowledge and his fellow beings' common culture ... a child with his own inclination and power to learn, investigate and develop as a human being in an active relation to other people ... a child who wants to take an active part in the knowledge-creating process, a child who in interaction with the world around is also active in the construction, in the creation of himself, his personality and his talents. This child is seen as having 'power over his own learning processes' and having the right to interpret the world. (Dahlberg, 1997: 22)

This image of the child, and related ideas about knowledge and learning, draws on social constructionist theories (for example, Berger and Luckman (1966), Gergen and Gergen (1991) and Maturana (1991)):

> In a social constructionist perspective, phenomena in the world around (environment) are seen as socially constructed phenomena and man as an active and creative subject. This way of thinking contains the emancipatory potential which means that we as human beings, as actors in our own lives, can change ourselves through our actions and in the power of the result of our actions (ibid: 21).

Similar views are expressed in many official documents. As early as 1972, a governmental committee on child care services (SOU,1972) stressed the dialogue pedagogical method. This view informs both the recent national curriculum and the training and education of staff. The official educational perspective is that children are 'actors', that is active participants in and constructors of their own development, including knowledge and identity.

How is the teacher perceived in this 'new' way of seeing things? As part of a book written by researchers, to mark the transfer (in 1998) of responsibility for early childhood services from the National Board of Health and Social Welfare to the National Agency for Education, Dahlberg (1997) writes on this subject:

> The view of the child as co-constructor implies a view of the teacher as co-constructor of culture and knowledge. This view means a twofold professional responsibility, which partly is about going into a dialogue and communicative action with the child, the group of children and colleagues, partly about a reflecting and researching attitude in which the starting point is the work and learning process of both the children and the teacher ... The teacher can have many different roles. Sometimes ... to direct: to present a problem and initiate work around preplanned material, or to introduce a new field of knowledge, to progress work further. Sometimes you are reduced to being a prompter and an assistant in a process which the children, by their own power, have initiated and direct by themselves ... The work of the teacher is mainly to be able to listen, see and let oneself

be inspired by and learn from what the children say and do. (23).

Birgitta Qvarsell also represents a child-centred view but in a somewhat different way. She too views children as agents of their own learning and their own development. In several reports, she problematises the concepts of 'children's needs', 'the best for children' and 'children's rights' and shows that they reveal different views on children:

> There is a tendency that 'children's needs' are interpreted from restricting theoretical constructs of what ought to be children's needs, from the view point of psychology. This might in turn lead to a focus on imaginary children rather than attention to real children and their actual as well as theoretical rights (Qvarsell, Dovelius and Eriksson, 1996: 29).

Together with Anna Eriksson and Johan Dovelius, Birgitta Qvarsell formed a research group, FOLK which, from 1995, has monitored a project – Research and learning in the local community – directed by the Swedish national road administration. Some 70 schools work thematically and generatively with questions about society, road transportation, traffic and environment. Methods are developed for children to investigate, describe, and analyse phenomena in the local community. In the project, attention is paid to both child and grown-up perspectives:

> One distinction that can be interesting – especially in connection with the school ... is the distinction between what teachers plan and what children do with what is planned.

Nowadays it is a well known phenomenon in educational research that what teachers intend to teach or perform does not always, perhaps even seldom, correspond to the way the pupils apprehend and above all carry out what was planned. [W]hen people (children and grown-ups) construct knowledge they use different kinds of available experiences, what is taught will be coded, people sift and choose, filter and decode, so that what comes out at the 'other end' ... often has little in common with the teaching content. It has been reconstructed. (Qvarsell et al., 1996: 31)

These are only some examples of the ways of thinking about children developing in Sweden (see also, for example, the contributions by Hultqvist and Dencik in Dahlgren and Hultqvist, 1995; and also Pramling, 1998). They have in common the potential to inform pedagogies which place children at the centre of their own learning, and so make the school a place in which children are not marginalised, but central, participants. They may not be universally accepted, nor are they fully embodied in practice, but they are already making an important contribution to the shaping of practice.

The rights of the child

This centrality of children is to be seen, also, in the measures arising from Sweden's ratification of the UN Convention on the Rights of the Child (SFS 1993:710; amended 1996:621) and in the appointment of a Children's Ombudsman (*Barnombudsmannen*, or BO). One of the tasks of the BO is to be proactive in questions concerning the rights and interests of children and young people, and the obligations of Sweden under the Convention. Among the BO's other duties is to make an annual report to the government. In the third report, *Childhood makes traces* (Barnombudsmannen, 1997), the BO put forward concrete suggestions and opinions to the government: to increase the influence of children and young people in issues concerning them, including bullying, the UN convention as it is operationalised at the local authority level, children's services, sexual abuse and child security at home. In *Small gets big* (Barnombudsmannen, 1998) the results of a survey of 1,600 pupils, age 10, conducted by Statistics Sweden showed that most were content:

> Everything is not a problem. Everything is not misery. Most children in the fourth year of school say that they feel safe and secure. They like school. And their spare time. They get on well in their everyday life, with friends, in the football team, in the drama group and so on. But this does not make it less important to deal with those problems that nevertheless exist. (Barnombudsmannen, 1998: 9)

Lisbeth Flising writes, in her review for this report, that the

> UN Children's Convention is a burning issue in Sweden and has initiated many projects and investigations. The government put forward a proposition (Prop 1997/98: 182) entitled Strategy to realize the UN Convention on the Rights of Children in Sweden.

The government has reserved 20 million SEK (about £2 million) to support the work of voluntary organisations to investigate and to implement the convention. For example ENSAC Sweden has a project on investigating how local authorities have adopted the UN Convention in order to make a better life for their children.

Issues and conclusion

The Swedish school seems to be becoming a community institution, complex and potentially potent, which functions as a local network and a site for different modes of learning by professionals, parents and children. The learning is accomplished through dialogue, relationships and the individual actions and explorations which are supported by these. The child is at the centre, a learning child within a learning community, rather than the recipient of already processed knowledge handed down from adults. The processes proposed for the school are seen as relational, based on dialogue between different professionals, between users (children and parents) and professionals, and between users. The relational approach is also apparent within the pedagogies of the integrated school, whether relating to free time or to the classroom. It may be perceived, also, within understandings of support for pupils and parents and the practices, such as the developmental conversation, which relate to these. At the same time, respect for the individual child or adult, as an active constructor of knowledge and of their own development, is balanced by notions of co-construction and collective responsibility.

At a structural level, legislation has underpinned children's inclusion in services as a matter of right; administrative integration has supported a new relationship between schools and other services; and decentralisation has produced mechanisms which facilitate parents and children's participation in decision making about the school.

Swedish informants would report that none of

the above developments is perfectly achieved, and the research reported here shows that there is still some way to go. Nevertheless, the case of Sweden presents a clear example of a country where there is ongoing public debate about children and childhood, parents and parenthood; where the dominant discourse on these is transparent and based on notions of a society where 'social exclusion' is not a major concern; and where the better working of democracy is given prominence in law and in the administration and operation of children's services.

Key themes and features

- a rich and developing debate on children and childhood, with children seen as active participants in their own learning and co-constructors of knowledge
- emphasis on UN Convention on the Rights of the Child
- developments in children's participation in decision making at school, extending to the content of education
- an extensive system of publicly-funded, professionally staffed, coordinated education and child care for children aged 1 to 12 years, including free time services for school children with integration of services within the education system and often within schools themselves
- new ways of working and growing collaboration between school teachers and other groups of staff, often within the classroom
- process evaluations point to the necessity for forward planning, good team work, energetic leadership and suitable premises
- decentralisation from central to local government and thence, in part, to parents
- emphasis on parental (and inter parental) support, and participation in decision making, rather than parental education

---

5 Conclusions

Focus and rationale

Within very different contexts, work is underway in France, the US and Sweden on relationships between schools, families and communities. There are, however, major differences in the focus and rationale of this work.

Initiatives in the US are mainly targeted at particular areas or groups considered to be at 'high risk'. The hope is that such initiatives can reverse increasing economic inequality and social dislocation. There is great diversity across programmes and initiatives, reflecting a more general diversity in services and policies due in part to the particular forms taken by the government and welfare state in the US. Much attention is paid to different types of collaboration between services and agencies, less to structural change in the relationships between them.

Swedish developments are not targeted, but rather concerned with reforming and extending a system of services with a strong tradition of universal provision. They include structural reform, for example the integration of responsibility for different services and the development of an integrated day for children containing elements of schooling, care, recreation and other activities – all this within a strong discourse on democracy, participation and children's rights. Issues of social exclusion are not prominent, perhaps because other policies have prevented or mitigated processes of inequality and dislocation.

France comes somewhat in between. On the one hand, a more integrated day for all children is under development, which engages a range of widely available services and activities. But on the other hand, there are programmes targeted at disadvantaged areas, which include measures to promote closer school-family-community relationships. French developments take place within the framework of a strong set of republican values emphasising citizenship, equality, secularity and culture.

Many ways forward

Both within and between countries, new work on the relationship between school, family and community covers many different areas. It varies greatly in terms of where it is located, its content, purpose and the nature of the relationships involved. Relationships between schools and other services range from informal networks and arrangements, through different types of coordination, partnership and collaborations, to actual integration.

Another parameter of diversity highlighted by this review is the nature of the relationship between the school, parents and children. At one level, this concerns 'openness'. How easy is it for parents to approach and enter the school in the course of its normal operation? At another level, this concerns power and rights. On what basis do children and parents use services, for example, by universal entitlement or because they are 'in need'? What power do children and parents have over decision-making (emphasised more by Sweden than France or the US)?

What works?

No country has convincing results from evaluations located within the 'input-output' paradigm. Even in the US, where such evaluation is most valued, the jury is out on two counts: whether such interventions 'work' (and if so, at what cost), and to what extent generalisable conclusions can be drawn from evaluations of particular projects in what is a 'complex and inherently messy field'.

Structural changes

Some of the complexity of the field is removed when there is recourse to restructuring, rather than the encouragement of partnerships between agencies. Structural changes in Sweden, at local and national level, have brought early childhood and free-time services alongside the school, all within the education system. Similar restructuring is not apparent in the US or France, at any level – although in France school-age child care and aspects of free-time services are commonly organised within the structures of the school.

The restructuring and extension of services has implications for staffing. In Sweden the three main professions for working with children are all well trained and relatively well paid. Preschool and school teachers and free-time pedagogues work increasingly closely together as services increasingly work closer together, totally integrating in some cases. There are even discussions about whether these different professions might be merged into a single pedagogical profession. By contrast, in both France and the US staffing remains more fragmented, with differing levels of training and status, and with no apparent rethinking of roles and structures.

The future of the school

Schools are the largest, most highly resourced and most deeply entrenched of public services for children and families. They face increasing demands as societies look to them as agents of social redemption and economic success. It is perhaps not surprising, therefore, that some educationists query (at least in the US) whether schools should become involved with non-academic activities, rather than focusing on their 'academic mission'. A recurrent theme, also, is the resistance of schools to change. Can this be broken down, and if so how? If schools take on a wider range of activities and services, how do we conceptualise (indeed name) schools? Do they remain 'schools', with all the connotations and implications of that name, or might they transform themselves into another sort of 'children's service', with a name that reflects a broader remit and concern? Does 'school inclusion' imply an expansion of the empire of the school, a process of takeover, or might it mean the transformation of schools into something new?

Underlying these questions is a sense of unease about the school becoming a means of organising and controlling all aspects of children's lives, a panoptical institution in which children are continually in the adult gaze and processed to produce an array of outputs predetermined by adults? This unease is occasionally articulated, for example in the Norwegian Government's *Framework Plan for Barnehager* (kindergartens) which refers to the importance of children's 'free space' being protected, 'to ensure that their lives are not totally controlled by adults' (BFD, 1996). Does attention also need to be given to creating or maintaining spaces for children and children's culture, less affected by adult agendas and attempts at organising children's lives?

Children and childhood

In our view, rethinking the relationship between school, family and community also means rethinking schools and other services for children – their purposes, their administration and legislation (at national and local levels) and the structure of staffing. And this in turn requires rethinking children and childhood, and seeking an answer to Mog Ball's concluding question in her *School Inclusion* report (1998): 'Is a completely new approach to childhood, perhaps based on the UN Convention on the Rights of the Child, necessary?' (58).

This review has clearly shown how concepts and practices are produced from particular discourses about, and constructions of, children and childhood. For example, Sweden and the US have quite different policy agendas, not just because their economic and social conditions are different, but because as societies they understand children and childhood differently. That is why we have emphasised from the beginning the need to combine a legitimate concern with effectiveness (management and measurement) with an equally legitimate concern with values, in particular an awareness of the ethical issue involved in how we **choose** to understand childhood and the relationship between children, family, local community and wider society.

Recent years have witnessed a strong development in Britain of the related fields of children's rights and childhood studies. This development places emphasis on children as social actors and members of a social group – a minority group – with their own interests, cultures, voices and rights, occupying a place in society as well as the family, and on childhood as an important stage in the life course, of value in its own right. This 'new paradigm of the sociology of childhood' (James and Prout, 1997) has led to a growing body of literature and research (such as the Economic

and Social Research Council's current research programme, Childhood 5–16). This British work has been influenced by Scandinavian work on childhood which, in turn, has influenced public policy in Scandinavian countries (see, for example, the chapter on Sweden).

Yet this work on childhood has had little impact on the wider field of public policy in Britain, where ideas about children and childhood seem to owe more to the 'developmental' and 'empty box' models that predominate in the US; policy documents can be searched in vain for any substantive discussion of the child or childhood. The discussion of 'school inclusion' or, more broadly the relationship between school, children, families and communities would benefit from dialogue with the field of childhood studies and the new perspectives that such dialogue would bring to that discussion. The inclusion of childhood studies, together with maintaining strong Scandinavian as well as American links, would help place debates about school inclusion in relation to a wider range of critical questions, not only 'what works?', but also 'who do we think children are?', 'what do we want for our children, here and now (as children) and in the future?', 'what is a good childhood?', 'what is children's relationship to and place in society?' and 'what are the purposes of institutions for children?'

Sweden also points to the relationship between constructions of the child and understandings of concepts such as 'learning' and 'knowledge'. It would be instructive to go beyond existing cross-national comparisons of academic attainment to examine how 'learning' and 'knowledge' are understood and discussed in different societies, and the implications for relationships between school, child, family and community. One interesting implication, again raised in the Swedish chapter, is that activities such as 'parent education' or 'parent support' might have quite different meanings depending on whether they were seen as transmitting a body of 'proven' knowledge (for example, child development) to parents or parents constructing their own knowledge, including their own understandings of their children, through active participation in processes such as pedagogical documentation (Dahlberg et al., 1999). At the very least, when making cross-national comparisons, we need to recognise that terms such as 'learning', 'knowledge', 'pedagogy' and 'education' carry different meanings in different societies, and different implications for practice.

Employment and time

Why is the issue of 'school inclusion' – or the relationship between school, family and community – reappearing now? Part of the explanation is as a response to a profound sense of unease about the state of our societies, especially the condition of our children, young people and families. This unease has been particularly acute in the US and the UK, countries which have experienced greatly increased inequality, insecurity and instability in recent years. Deteriorating conditions for many children and families seem related to economic changes gathering pace since the late 1970s, and increasingly manifest in labour market participation (for example, increasing unemployment and numbers of 'workless' families) and employment patterns and practice (for example, increasing concentration, intensification and insecurity of paid work). The same concerns and changes can be seen in all countries, but not as yet in such extreme forms as the US and the UK, which have been at the forefront of embracing neo-liberal market economics with its attendant values of competition, flexibility and individualisation.

Renewed interest in 'school inclusion' may be affected by, as well as an effect of, employment change. We seem to face a paradox: parents are being urged to become more involved with their children and their schools, while at the same time many have less time and energy available for involvement because of their employment. Given such circumstances, is 'school inclusion' addressed, in practice, to parents with marginal involvement in the labour market and to their children? Is that its intention? If not, and if it is addressed to all parents and children, then what conditions may enable parents to be involved? For example, Swedish parents not only have shorter working weeks and longer holiday entitlements than American parents, but are entitled to a range of leave entitlements related to parenthood, ranging from parental leave to time off work to care for sick children, all paid. We notice also that in France parents elected to various educational councils have the right to take time off work in order to participate.

Yet despite the increasing centrality of employment to parenthood and childhood, the review has found few references that enquire into the issue, and its consequences for school-child-parent-community relationships. Indeed, for recognition of the issue we have to turn to an American study of the relationship between work and home in one particular community. Hochschild (1997) concludes that

> libraries, childcare centers, schools, houses of worship and after-school programs were relying on a dwindling bands of 'old regulars' to help with outings, new projects, and

fundraising ... [T]he proportion of Americans reporting that they had attended a public meeting on town or school affairs in the previous year fell from 22 per cent in 1973 to 13 per cent in 1993 ... Membership in Parent-Teacher Associations, the League of Women Voters, the Red Cross, the Boy Scouts, the Lions Clubs, the Elks, the Jaycees, the Masons, and most other civic organisations has also fallen.

Should we conclude, then, that the time bind is leading us toward not only the parent-free home, but also the participant-free civic society and the citizen-free democracy? If the question were put to them in this way, most ... parents [in the study] – still dreaming of potential communities inhabited by potential selves – might reluctantly agree and shake their heads in disapproval (243–4)

This points to the need for a broader and more thoughtful questioning of what is going on in the relationship between economic, labour market and employment change, and change in family life and parenting. Any consideration of school inclusion must be informed by the results of such questioning, not to mention questioning of our understanding of childhood and education. We hope that this report indicates something of these matters and the value of taking a cross-national perspective, both for framing questions and for throwing light on the many possible choices that may be available when seeking answers to these questions.

References

Adelman, H. S. and Taylor, L. (1997) 'Addressing barriers to learning: beyond school-linked services and full-service schools', *American Journal of Orthopsychiatry*, 67 (3).

Adler, L. (1993) 'Introduction and Overview to Special Issue', *Journal of Educational Policy*, 8, 1–16.

Baker, B. (1998) '"Childhood" in the emergence and spread of the US public school', in Popkewitz, T. and Brennan, M. (Eds.) *Foucault's Challenge: Discourse, Knowledge and Power in Education*. New York: Teachers College Press

Ball, M. (1998) *School Inclusion: The School, the Family and the Community*. York: Joseph Rowntree Foundation

Barnombudsmannen (The Children's Ombudsman) (1997) *Barndom sätter spår. Rapport från barnens myndighe (Childhood makes traces, Report from the children's authorities)*. Stockholm: Barnombudsmannen

Barnombudsmannen (The Children's Ombudsman) (1998) *Liten blir stor. Rapport från barnens myndighe (Small gets big. Report from the children's authorities)*. Stockholm: Barnombudsmannen

Bartley, K. (1998) *Barnpolitik och barnets rättigheter. (Child policy and the rights of the child)*. Dissertation at the University of Göteborg, Department of Sociology

Berger, P. and Luckman, T. (1966) *The Social Construction of Reality*. New York: Doubleday

BFD (Norwegian Ministry of Children and Family Affairs) (1996) *Framework Play for Day Care Institutions: A Brief Presentation*. Oslo: BFD

Boyd, W. L. (1998a) 'Competing models of schools and communities: the struggle to reframe and reinvent their relationships', Internet website: www.temple.edu/LSS: Laboratory for Student Success.

Boyd, W. L. (1998b) 'The "loyal opposition" and the future of British and US school reform', Internet website: www.temple.edu/LSS: Laboratory for Student Success.

Bradshaw, J., Kennedy, S., Kilkey, M., Hutton, S., Corden, A., Eardley, T., Holmes, H. and Neale, J. (1996) *Policy and the Employment of Lone Parents in 20 Countries*. York: Social Policy Research Unit, University of York

Brown, C. and Hara, S. (1999) *State Education Agency Support for School-community Collaboration in the Mid-Atlantic States*. National Invitational Conference on Improving Results for Children and Families by Connecting Collaborative Services with School Reform Efforts, Washington, DC, Laboratory for Student Success, Temple University Center for Research in Human Development and Education.

Casper, L.M., Hawkins, M. and O'Connell, M. (1994) *Who's Minding the Kids? Childcare arrangements: Fall 1991 (U.S. Bureau of the Census, Current Population Reports, p.70–36)*, Washington, D.C.: U.S. Government Printing Office

Chambon, A. and Proux, M. 'Ecole et communauté éducative', in Zay, D. and Gonnin-Bolo, A. (Eds.), *Etablissements et partenariats: stratégies pour un projet commun. Actes de colloques*, Janvier 1993

References

Cherryholmes, C. (1988) *Power and Criticism: Poststructural Investigations in Education.* New York: Teachers College Press

Cincotta, H, Holden, R. and Givens, D. (1986) *The United States System of Education.* Washington D.C.: US Information Agency

Combes, J.(1998) 'Parental involvement in preschool education in France', in *Children and families at risk: New issues in integrating service.* Paris: OECD

Coppey, O. (1993) 'Partenariat et apprentissage, les musées et les IUFM', in Zay, D. and Gonnin-Bolo, A. (Eds.), *Etablissements et partenariats: stratégies pour un projet commun. Actes de colloques,* Janvier 1993

Crowson, R. L. and. Boyd, W. L. (1996) 'Achieving coordinated school-linked services: facilitating utilization of the emerging knowledge base.' *Educational Policy,* 10(2): 253-272.

Dahlberg, G. (1997) 'Barnet och pedagogen som medkonstruktorer av kultur och kunskap' ('The child and the pedagogue as co-constructors of culture and knowledge'), in *Roster om den svenska barnomsorgen. SoS-rapport 1997:23 (Voices about Swedish child care, SOS-report 1997:23).* Stockholm: Socialstyrelsen (National Board of Health and Social Welfare)

Dahlberg, G., Moss, P. and Pence, A. (1999) *Beyond Quality in Early Childhood Education and Care: Postmodern Perspectives.* London: Falmer Press

Dahlgren, L. and Hultqvist, K. (Eds.) (1995) *Seeendet och seeendet s villkor – En bok om barns och ungas välfärd. (The seeing and the conditions of seeing – A book about the welfare of children and young people).* Stockholm: HLS Förlag

DeWitt Wallace-Reader's Digest Fund (1999) 'An Overview of the Extended-Service Schools Initiative'.

Driscoll, M. E., Boyd, W. L. et al. (1998) 'Collaborative Services Initiatives: A Report of a National Survey of Programs.' Internet website: www.temple.edu/LSS: Laboratory for Student Success.

Dryfoos, J. G. (1994) 'Policy point of view: conceptualizing new institutions – full service schools.' News and Issues: National Center for Children in Poverty Winter/Spring Issue.

Esping-Andersen, G. (1990) *The Three Worlds of Welfare Capitalism.* Cambridge: Polity Press

Eurostat (1999) *Living conditions in Europe: Statistical Pocketbook.* Luxembourg: Office for Official Publicationa of the European Communities

Flising, B. (1995) *Samverkan skola-skolbarnsomsorg, SoS-rapport 1995:12. (Cooperation school – school-age child care, SoS-report 1995:12),* Stockholm: Socialstyrelen (National Board of Health and Social Welfare)

Flising, L., Fredriksson, G. and Lund, K. (1996): *Föräldrakontakt – en bok om att skapa, behålla och utveckla ett gott föräldrasamarbet. (Parent involvement – a book about creating, keeping and developing good parent cooperation).* Stockholm: Informationsförlaget

Gergen, K. J. and Gergen, M. M. 'Towards Reflexive

Methodologies', in Steier, F. (Ed) *Research and Reflexivity.* London: Sage

Hansen, M. (1999) *Yrkeskulturer i möte. Läraven fritidspedagogen och samverken. (Collaboration between two teaching cultures. Teachers, free-time pedagogues and cooperation).* PhD thesis, University of Göteborg.

Hatch. J.A. (1995) 'Studying childhood as a cultural invention: a rationale and framework', in J.A. Hatch (Ed.), *Qualitiative Research in Early Childhood Settings.* Westport. Conn.: Praeger

Hertert, L. (1996) 'Systemic school reform in the 1990s: a local perspective', *Educational Policy* 10 (3): 379.

Hochschild, A. (1997) *The Time Bind: When Work becomes Home and Home becomes Work.* New York: Metropolitan Books

Hocquard, D. (1993) 'Des enseignants regardent l'entreprise', in D. Zay and A. Gonnin-Bolo (Eds.) *Etablissements et partenariats: stratégies pour un projet commun. Actes de colloques,* Janvier 1993

Honig, M. I. and Jehl, J. D. (1999) *Toward a Federal Support System for Connecting Educational Improvement Strategies and Collaborative Services.* National Invitational Conference on Improving Results for Children and Families by Connecting Collaborative Services with School Reform Efforts, Washington, DC, Laboratory for Student Success, Temple University Center for Research in Human Development and Education.

Hutton, W. (1995) *The State We're In.* London: Jonathan Cape

James, A., Jenks, C. and Prout, A. (1998) *Theorizing Childhood.* Cambridge: Polity Press

James A. and Prout, A. (Eds.) (1997) *Constructing and Deconstructing Childhood: Contemporary Issues in the Sociological Study of Childhood* (Second Edition). London: Falmer Press

Kagan, S. (1997) 'Support Systems for Children, Youths, Families, and Schools in Inner-city situations.' *Education and Urban Society* 29 (3): 277–295.

Koppich, J. E. and Kirst, M.W. (1993) 'Editors' introduction to special issue of Education and Urban Society', *Education and Urban Society* 25 (2): 123–128.

Kristoffersson, M. (1998) *Föräldrasamverkan 'Lokala styrelser' – är det en bra modell för inflytande? (Parent cooperation "local boards" – are they a good model for influence?)* Nordic Association for Educational Research, Lathi, Finland, 1998

Lallias, J-C. (1993) 'Le partenariat artistique dans le domaine du théâtre', in D. Zay and A. Gonnin-Bolo (Eds.) *Etablissements et partenariats: stratégies pour un projet commun. Actes de colloques,* Janvier 1993

Leseve-Nicolle, C. (1994) 'L'aménagement des rythmes de vie de l'enfant et du jeune', in *Journée de la Famille, 22 Septembre 1994, Actes du Colloque, 'L'accueil et le temps libre de jeunes enfants'*

Lpfö-98 (1998) *Läroplan för förskolan (Curriculum for the preschool).* Stockholm: Utbildningsdepartementet och Fritzes (Ministry of Education and Science)

Lpo-94 (1994) *Läroplan för det obligatoriska skolväsendet,*

References

förskoleklassen och fritidshemmet. (Curriculum for compulsory schools, preschool class and school-age free time). Stockholm: Utbildnings-departementet och Fritzes (Ministry of Education and Science)

Manning, J. B. and Rodriguez, L. (1999) Community for Learning: Connection with Community Services (Draft: Not for distribution), Office of Educational Research and Improvement of the U.S. Department of Education through a contract to the Mid-Atlantic Laboratory for Student Success (LSS) established at the Temple University Center for Research in Human Development and Education (CRHDE).

Marx, I. (1999) 'Low pay and Poverty in OECD countries', *Employment Audit,* 10, 17–21

Maturana, H. R. (1991) 'Science and daily life: the ontology of scientific explanations', in Steier, F. (Ed) *Research and Reflexivity.* London: Sage

Meijvogel, R. (1991) *Geen kruimels tussen de boeken: Schooltijden, overblijven en deontwikkeling van buitenschoolse opvang in Nederland.* Groningen: Ph.D. published thesis.

Melaville, A. I. and Blank, M.J. (1999) *Trends and Lessons in School-Community Initiatives.* National Invitational conference on Improving Results for Children and Families by Connecting Collaborative Services with School Reform Efforts, Washington, DC, Laboratory for Student Success, Temple University Center for Research in Human Development and Education.

Merseth, K. K., Schorr, L. B., et al. (1999) *Schools, Community-based Interventions, and Children's Learning and Development: What's the Connect?* National Invitational Conference on Improving Results for Children and Families by Connecting Collaborative Services with School Reform Efforts, Washington, DC, Laboratory for Student Success, Temple University Center for Research in Human Development and Education.

Mickleson, R.A. and Wadsworth, (1996) 'NASDC's Odyssey in Dallas (NC): Women, Class, and School Reform, *Educational Policy,* 10 (3), 315–341.

Ministère de la Jeunesse et des Sports (1992) *Analyse quantitative et qualitative des contrats ville-enfant et des contrats ville-enfant-jeune, Année scolaire 1991/92.*

Ministère de l'Education National de la Jeunesse et des Sports (1988) *Annexe de Prof. Hubery Montagner, lettre du 2 août 1988.*

Ministère de la Jeunesse et des Sports (1996) *Aménagement des Rhythms Scolaire, Strasbourg, 27 August, 1996*

Moss, P. and Petrie, P. (1997) *Children's Services: Time for a New Approach,* London: Institute of Education University of London

National Center for Education Statistics (1997) *Schools serving family needs: extended-day programs in public and private schools.* Washington D.C.: US Department of Education, Office of Educational Research and Improvement.

OECD (Organisation for Economic Cooperation and Development) (1997a) *Education at a Glance: OECD indicators 1997.* Paris: OECD

OECD (Organisation for Economic Cooperation and Development) (1997b) 'United States', in *Parents as Partners in Schooling*. Paris: OECD

OECD (Organisation for Economic Cooperation and Development) (1997c) 'France', in *Parents as Partners in Schooling*. Paris: OECD

OECD (Organisation for Economic Cooperation and Development) (1998) *OECD in Figures: Statistics on the Member Countries (1998 Edition)*. Paris: OECD

Payzant, T. W. (1992) 'New beginnings in San Diego: developing a strategy for interagency collaboration', *Phi Delta Kappan* 74 (2): 139.

Popkewitz, T. (1998) 'The culture of redemption and the administration of freedom in educational research', *The Review of Educational Research*, Spring, 1-35.

Pramling, I. (1998) *Att lära barn lära (Teaching children to learn)*, Acta Universitatis Gothoburgensis (Göteborg studies in educational sciences), 70

Prop 1997/98:182 *Strategi för att förverkliga FN:s konvention om barnets rättigheter i Sverige (Strategy for carrying out the UN Convention on the Rights of the Child in Sweden)*

Qvarsell, B., Dovelius, J. and Eriksson, A. (1996) *Att forska och lära i närsamhället Nya läromönster – nya arenor? FOLK-projektet rapport nr 1 (Researching and learning in the local community. New educational patterns – new scenes of action?* FOLK project report no.1). Stockholm: Pedagogiska institutionen, Stockholms Universitet (Department of Education, University of Stockholm)

Ritchey, E. (1998) *Föräldrar – är det nåt att ha? (Parents – what good are they?)* Stockholm: Skolverket (National Agency for Education)

Rohlin, M. (1997) *Arbetslaget – en källa till inspiration i Röster om den svenska barnomsorgen, SoS-rapport 1997:23 (The Work Team – a source of inspiration in Voices about Swedish child care SoS report 1997:23)*. Stockholm: Socialstyrelsen (National Board of Health and Social Welfare)

Sennett, R. (1998) *The Corrosion of Character.* New York and London: Norton

Seppanen, P.S et al (1993) *National Study of Before- and After-School Programs: Final Report*. Washington D.C.: U.S. Department of Education, Office of Policy and Planning.

SFS 1993:710 (revised 1996:621)

Smylie, M. A. and Crowson, R.L. (1996). 'Working within the scripts: building institutional infrastructure for children's service coordination in schools', *Educational Policy* 10 (1): 3-21.

SOU (1972:26-27) *Barnstugeutredningen (Government committee on child care).*

SOU (1974: 53) Skolans arbetsmiljö (The inner work of school)

SOU (1995:103) *Föräldrar i självförvaltande skolor Delbetänkande av Skolkommittén (Parents in self-administered schools. Interim report from the School Committee)*

References

SOU (1997:121) *Skolfrågor – Om skola i en ny tid. Slutbetänkande av Skolkommittén School matters – About school in a new age. Final report from the School Committee)*

SOU (1997:161) *Stöd i föräldraskapet. Betänkande av Utredningen om föräldrautbildning (Support in parenthood. Report from the Committee on Parent Education)*

SOU 1996:22 *Inflytande på riktigt – Om elevers rätt till inflytande, delaktighet och ansvar (Influence for real – About pupils' rights of influence, participation and responsibility)*

SOU 1996:143 *Krock eller möte – Om den mångkulturella skolan (Crash or meeting – About the multicultural school)*

Tham, A. (1998) *Jag vill ha inflytande över allt (I want to have influence over everything).* Stockholm: Skolverket (National Agency for Education)

U.S. Department of Education (1998) *Safe and Smart: Making the After-School Hours Work for Kids.* Washington, D.C.: Department of Education and Department of Justice.

Wang, M. C., Haertel, G. D. and Walberg, H. J. (1998) *The Effectiveness of Collaborative School-Linked Services,* Internet web site: www.temple.edu/LSS: Laboratory for Student Success.

Warren, C. (1999) 'Lessons from the Evaluation of New Jersey's School-based Youth Services Program. National Invitational Conference on Improving Results for Children and Families by Connecting Collaborative Services with School Reform Efforts, Washington, DC, laboratory for Student Success, Temple University Center for Research in Human Development and Education.

Wynn, J., Meyer, S. and Richards-Schuster, K (1999) *Furthering Education: The relationship of Schools and Other Organizations.* National Invitational conference on Improving Results for Children and Families by Connecting Collaborative Services with School Reform Efforts, Washington, DC, Laboratory for Student Success, Temple University Center for Research in Human Development and Education.

Zigler, E. S. and Lang, M. L. (1991) *Child-care Choices: Balancing the Needs of Children, Families and Society.* New York: Free Press